The Complete Guide to the Golden Retriever

Second Edition

Dedicated to my wife, Cynthia,
with whom I have shared the
happiness and friendships that
our Goldens have brought us

Acknowledgements are due to The Putman Publishing Group
for permission to reprint an extract from James Lamb Free's
Training Your Retriever.

Cover photograph and training photographs by Diana Ewings

Cover: From left to right. Bryanstown Avondale, Bryanstown
    Ingerid, Bryanstown Arainn Mhor, Pondcroft Sean of
    Bryanstown

THE COMPLETE GUIDE TO THE GOLDEN RETRIEVER

Second Edition

Michael Twist

PERRY GREEN PRESS

© Michael Twist 1999
First published by Boydell and Brewer 1988
Second edition published 1999 by Perry Green Press, Sudbury, Suffolk

British Library Cataloguing in Publication Data
A catalogue record for this book is available from the British Library.

ISBN: 1 902481 08 9

Printed in Great Britain by
Redwood Books, Trowbridge, Wiltshire

CONTENTS

FOREWORD

I am very pleased to be asked to write the foreword for the second edition of this book, something I did when it was first published ten years ago. Much remains the same. In fact all that on the subject of training is unchanged. The author requires a gundog to be able to mark, get out, hunt and find game without the constant use of the whistle and direction from the handler, which, at so many field trials these days, seems to be all the vogue with the handlers who have entered the sport via working tests.

This book has, for more than ten years, been a most useful adjunct to many in the breed and will continue to be so for those newcomers with a desire to succeed. Michael Twist with a wealth of experience and knowledge of the breed, gained over a period of more than fifty years, guides the beginner, from choosing a puppy through all the stages of development and training, whether the puppy is for work, show, or indeed both, or just as a pet and through to the use of stud dogs and whelping bitches. The section on gundog training explains in detail how to set about the task and, most importantly, what to do when things do not go according to plan, an aspect often ignored in books on training.

The conformation, character and temperament of Golden Retrievers is fully covered, as is showing, field trialing, the show gundog working certificate and working tests. The original book gave a very concise résumé on the often confusing aspects of hereditary diseases, in particular those affecting the eyes. Since then more conditions have been added to the BVA Eye Scheme and the author feels that, in their effort to obtain clear certificates for these defects, some people are forgetting the all-important issue of temperament, as well as breed, type and working ability. The chapter on this subject has therefore been completely re-written in an attempt to clarify what is becoming an ever increasing source of frustration and bewilderment, not only to novices, but also to many long established breeders.

In addition to a reappraisal on the hereditary diseases covered by BVA/KC Schemes and a general updating of a number of factors, there is an interesting addition about the possible origin of the breed, being an excerpt from Charles Gunter's *Gun-Room Brevities*, published by Spottiswoode 1882, which again makes a Russian connection. The Appendix has been updated and contains a proto-type of a Condition of Sale based on various elements of The Sale of Goods Act, from which both buyer and seller can draw up their own conditions. The prototype is not put forward as a watertight legal document, but purely as a guide for reference only. There are a number of additional photographs of dogs which have appealed to the author in the interim period between the book first being published and this new edition.

The author and his wife, Cynthia, have over a period of nearly fifty years, remained dedicated to dual-purpose Golden Retrievers; a fact born out by their record both in the show ring and field trials. When living in Ireland, they had in their kennel at the same time three Champions in the show ring, all of which were winners of Open Stake field trials. The most outstanding being Champion and Irish Champion Bryanstown Gale Warning, (eleven green stars and eleven challenge certificates) who must be the only Champion in the breed to finish fourth in a Retriever Championship (Ireland, 1970). To emphasise the author's dual-purpose approach, to what may now be described as almost a lifelong interest, in 1995 he judged the Golden Retriever dogs at Crufts and, later that year was one of the judges at the Golden Retriever Club's 24 dog Open Stake qualifying for the Retriever Championship – one cannot get much more dual-purpose than that!

Although this book was written primarily to aid beginners, there is much in it for everyone and I can confidently recommend it as a worthwhile addition to the bookshelf of anyone interested in Golden Retrievers, or, indeed, all working gundogs.

Joan M. Gill

Joan M. Gill.

Historical Note

For a number of years a certain mystery and romanticism surrounded the origin of this beautiful breed, the most popular story being that Lord Tweedmouth, whilst visiting Brighton, attended a circus where a troupe of some six to eight Russian dogs were performing. His Lordship was so fascinated by them, that he purchased the entire act and took them back to Guisachan House, his home in Invernesshire.

Another, less well known basis for their foundation, appears in Charles Gunter's book, *Gun-Room Brevities* (Spottiswoode 1882). He writes that one Captain Harry Hieover had his charger shot from under him at the battle of Balaclava. As he walked back to the British lines he passed a Russian gun, surrounded by the dead gun-crew, but, unhurt, sitting whimpering in their midst was a biggish, wavy coated, cream-coloured puppy. With a little persuasion the gallant captain got the puppy to accompany him, and on returning to camp he handed the dog over to his batman, Tom Spurrier, who christened his new charge 'Voddy'. He found the pup to be extremely intelligent and assured his *gentleman* that he could teach 'Voddy' things, as he put it, 'as easy as drink a pint'. Subsequently he declared, 'I'd be saying that there dog has the makings of a shooting-dog, sir, fetches and carries like egg-shells he do'. Voddy returned to England with ensign Sir Digby Wildrake, but was subsequently stolen. After the fall of Sevastopol the British troops returned to England. Tom Spurrier, once home, took his young lady to see a circus. High on the billing was 'Toots, the Canine Comedian'. When 'Toots' appeared Tom realised it was 'Voddy'. He whistled on his fingers – three staccato notes. 'Voddy' left the ring in a flash and, after much wrangling and the intervention of the police, 'Voddy' was returned to Captain Harry. Later in the year Captain Harry was hunting with Lord Wolverton's tan-and-golden hounds, who were noted for their scenting ability and the painstaking way they would puzzle out a line. The Captain had a great idea and obtained a draft bitch from Lord Wolverton's pack, which he mated to 'Voddy' and so, some believed, laid the foundation to the Golden Retriever breed. The origin of the breed was thoroughly researched by Elma Stonex, just before and after the last war. She was a famous breeder of Goldens and owner of the 'Dorcas' kennel and, for many years chairman of the Golden Retriever Club. One thing from the past which is certainly compatible with the facts, is the involvement of Lord Tweedmouth, which I will explain in a moment. However, I find it interesting, that in both versions, a circus is a central feature!

In 1854 Sir Dudley Coutts Marjoribank, who twelve years later became Lord Tweedmouth was staying at Guisachan House in Invernesshire, then owned by the Fraser family. He fell in love with the property and bought it. Not only was he keen on retrievers, for he certainly kept Pointers, Deerhounds and Cairn Terriers as well, but he, also, bred Aberdeen Angus cattle and ponies. In all cases it seems as though he kept careful records of the various matings of his dogs. In 1889 the Guisachan records show two yellow bitch puppies were born, and subsequently recorded as Prim and Rose. They were sired by the five year old dog, Nous 2nd, who the records show as being one of a litter of four yellow puppies. His great grandfather was also Nous. Lord Tweedmouth's records show that he, too, was a yellow retriever, bought in 1864 and died in 1872. The dam of Prim and Rose was a two year old black bitch, 'Queenie', one of a litter of ten. Her dam, Gill, was out of Zoe and by Jack. A similar mating to that which produced Nous 2nd. I would suggest to those who are seriously interested in the genealogy of the breed to obtain a copy of Valerie Foss's *The Golden Retriever. Second Book of Champions*, in which virtually all that is known regarding the origin of the breed is recorded. It would seem that Prim and Rose were the last yellow puppies bred by Lord Tweedmouth, for he died in 1894. One thing I find intriguing in Valerie Foss's book is where she says, 'The only Russian connection here could have been if the Earl of Chichester had fought in the 1853–1856 Crimean War and brought back an ancestor of Nous. That of course refers to the first Nous bought by Lord Tweedmouth in 1864 from the Earl of Chichester. One is therefore left wondering if there is any truth in the story about 'Voddy,' as recorded in Charles Gunter's *Gun-Room Brevities*. Voddy was but a pup in October 1854. It is by no means beyond the bounds of possibilities that he could have sired Nous or, possibly, have been his grandsire!

Ch Bryanstown Gaucho
(Sire Ch Stolford Happy Lad, dam Janacre Gaiety of Bryanstown)
BOB Crufts 1981. 18 CCs
Owner/Breeder Mr and Mrs M . F . Twist

1

Recollections and Food for Thought

Over the past fifty years since I first owned a Golden Retriever, sixty-seven since my first working gundog, a Cocker/Springer bitch, I have derived much pleasure from my dogs, be it in the shooting field, show ring, or just as devoted companions. The following chapters are written in the belief that the reader is truly a complete novice, but I would hope that much of the experience I have gained would help extend the knowledge of training and general welfare of Goldens for both the novice and established owner alike.

If your wish is to own a Golden for work, showing or just as a pet, some element of training is essential. Over the years I have read a great number of books on training, most of which have a common theme – 'if your dog does not come up to scratch, get rid of it'. One writer in the early part of the century even advocated shooting it! Easy enough to write, and indeed to put into practice. No, I don't mean shoot it, but find it a home as a pet. However, there is a snag. By the time you discover you have a dog that it seems you cannot train, the chances are that your Golden has become a much-loved member of the household. They have a habit of doing this, and their departure would cause, in many cases, a major domestic crisis. It would give me a great satisfaction if the following text helps to avert such a situation.

Before discussing the purchase of your puppy, let me say just a few words about the breed, which was originally evolved purely for work.

It was not until 1920 that the Kennel Club agreed to a separate register for Retrievers (Golden); prior to that they were registered as Retrievers (Golden or Yellow). In spite of that, the Golden Retriever Club was formed in 1913, very largely due to the enthusiasm and dedication of Mrs W. Charlesworth, just five years after the breed was first exhibited at a show. It was around 1910 or 1911 when Goldens first started to appear at field trials, but only in very limited numbers. Mrs Charlesworth was a lady of great charm, providing one kept the right side of her, a very knowledgeable, and a most outspoken and forceful character who left you in little doubt of her opinion of you or your dog. I well remember

1

spending a most educational couple of hours sitting with her at Crufts in the early 1950s. She pointed out the failings of many of the exhibits in a most stentorian voice and acclaimed their virtues with equal clarity. It seems incredible today, but I recall what happened when it was time for lunch and I left the ring. My wife and I accompanied Kit and Peter Fraser, of Westhyde fame, into the restaurant. We had no difficulty in getting a table and, would you believe it, when we returned to the judging ring there were plenty of empty seats! To return to Mrs Charlesworth, her Noramby Kennel played a major roll in establishing the breed. She produced many champions and they all worked. It was she who bred and exhibited the first Golden ever to achieve Champion status, namely her Champion Noramby Campfire.

The first Dual Champion, that is one that has attained its title in the show ring and also won the title of Field Trial Champion, was Captain Dick Hermon's Balcombe Boy. I had the privilege of being associated for a number of years with Captain Hermon when we both held office with the All-Ireland Golden Retriever Club, he as president, I as chairman.

For the benefit of the uninitiated, a Champion is a dog that has won three Challenge Certificates at Championship shows under three different judges and has won either a Field Trial award or a Working Certificate. If it has won neither, it is designated a Show Champion. A Field Trial Champion is a dog that has won two, or in some cases three, Open or All-Aged Stakes, one of which must have been open to all breeds of Retrievers. If one studies the show and field trial records just prior to the Second World War and immediately after, it will be seen that the same dogs frequently featured in both the Championship Show and Field Trial awards. What was then commonplace is now a rarity.

From the Golden Retriever Club's *Victory Year Book* of 1945–6, one learns that there were 393 members of the club at that time, fifty four of whom had registered prefixes. There are now fourteen specialist clubs encompassing many thousands of members! Few whose names appear in that memorable year book remain active within the breed, but there are some: Mr R Burnett (Rossbourne), Miss R. Clark (Rosecot), and Mrs Marion Dawson. There are no doubt more who were involved in the breed at that time but were not members of the club. One, for example, is Miss Joan Gill (Westley), who had Goldens in 1936 and had, at one time, one of the greatest kennels of dual-purpose Goldens there has ever been. She bred the only International Dual Champion, namely Miss Lucy Ross's David of Westley.

The early kennels, their achievements and breeding are well recorded in Mrs Joan Tudor's excellent book *The Golden Retriever* and also by Mrs Elma Stonex, who was the greatest authority on the genealogy of the breed. It was she who over more than ten years unstintingly researched its origin with the aid of the sixth Earl of Ilchester, and, in 1959, she came up with indisputable evidence about the source from which the Golden Retriever was bred and developed. This evidence was placed before the Kennel Club and was accepted.

I think it worthwhile to draw attention to the fact that, thanks to the work done by Mrs Stonex, the whole breed as it exists today can trace its origin back to four matings, that took place in the early 1920s. These were Glory of Fyning to Stagden Cross Pamela, Dual Champion Balcombe Boy to Balcombe Bunty, Binks of Kentford to Balvaig and Rory of Bentley to Aurora. The progeny from these unions were intermated and from those roots the breed expanded to become one of the largest in numbers and one of the most popular of those that exist today. Whether this popularity has been a benefit to the breed is very debatable; personally I think not. Unfortunately many people are of a rapacious nature; this has led to much indiscriminate breeding by those wishing to cash in on the popularity of the breed. So beware, we have our quota of charlatans out for the quick buck.

Alas, most of those who read this book will have already purchased their puppy. If you haven't, pay attention; I have a few do's and dont's for you.

Before you buy a puppy, if it is your first one, give the matter very careful consideration. I have found not infrequently that people meet a charming Golden and then it's a case of, 'Oh, we must get one.' Fair enough; this may work out ideally for all concerned, but buying a puppy on impulse can be disastrous. The most common example of this is where the owner is out at work all day. When you obtain your new acquisition it will be around 8 weeks old and should be having four feeds, one of these in the middle of the day. Apart from this, if it is to be house-trained, you must, obviously, be there to take it out at regular intervals. Irrespective of these practical points, there is the psychological effect on the puppy of leaving it alone all day; it needs companionship and love. Oh yes, you can leave a puppy alone all day, but at what cost? As the puppy grows it will become stronger and more active; it will also become bored and will begin to while away the time by chewing up anything that is available. You'll return tired from work and find messes and puddles all over the place and perhaps the leg of a chair half eaten through. You will blame the puppy and you will be wrong; it is you who will be at fault. How can the puppy know any better if you haven't been there to teach it? There are, of course, the ignoramuses who will return to a scene such as I have described, tired and irritable, and will grab the unfortunate puppy, rub its nose in the mess, push its mouth up against the chewed furniture, smack it and throw it out into the garden. The poor little thing hasn't a clue why it has been treated so harshly; it cannot correlate the action with its misdemeanour of quite possibly some hours before, but it will quickly learn that its owner is not a very nice person and is to be avoided whenever possible. There will be readers who will not believe that such stupidity can exist, but I can assure you that it does. So, quite simply, if you cannot give the time it requires to a puppy, don't buy one; wait until you can give the time.

Don't buy a puppy from a puppy farmer-cum-dealer. These are people who breed indiscriminately for sale, mating their bitches virtually every season, quite irrespective of their condition. They normally advertise fairly extensively and have a number of breeds on offer – when you see this, beware! The ones who are purely dealers buy in litters of puppies, many coming from farms in Wales. It is not uncommon for the premises of the dealers to be riddled with disease, their prices exorbitant and, not infrequently, for the pedigrees of the puppies to be suspect. Esther Rantzen has, on several occasions on *That's Life*, given excellent coverage and exposure to such establishments. Some years ago, I was able to assist in getting one such place closed. What a job it was, but eventually it was achieved. Before taking action we were able to get a spy into the premises and she had a good nose round before being discovered and ejected. What she found was horrific. Bitches with litters were being kept under the most appalling conditions. One Golden bitch with puppies was in a pit dug in the ground and covered with a few old pieces of corrugated iron sheeting. Dead puppies lay around all over the place and the filth and misery were unbelievable, yet it took several visits to court before this person was eventually put out of business and closed down for good. It may well be that there are dealers with premises that are well run, clean and free from disease. There is absolutely no reason why there shouldn't be but, alas, I have yet to come across one. Why take chances? There are plenty of reputable breeders.

Don't buy a puppy as a toy for the kids – it has feelings too! Certainly buy one as a friend and companion for them, but not as something that may be teased, pulled around and fought over. I well remember a charming couple booking a puppy. They had the time and the premises; in fact everything seemed fine. Yes, they had children. I gave them a long spiel on the relationship that should exist between the children and the puppy. They assured me that they quite understood. They called a couple of times between the initial visit and the day of collection to see the puppy. The day came for it to go and the would-be-owners arrived, plus their three kids. The latter tumbled out of the car rather like marauding Red Indians – I was not impressed. We went round to the kennel and I lifted out the puppy and handed it to the eldest child. What happened was like a Rugby football scrummage! The parents stood benignly looking on, giving not one word of admonishment. I went in over the top, rescued the pup and returned it to the kennel. The deal was off. The parents thought me most unreasonable!

Right, if you are satisfied that you can give a proper home to a puppy, let's proceed. The next thing to decide is whether you want just a pet, a show dog, a dual-purpose dog or purely a gundog. I appreciate that 'pet' may apply to the last three categories of dogs with another specific purpose in life. If your main requirement is a gundog – and I may remind you that we are talking about your first puppy – then I am sure you would expect me to advise going to a breeder specialising in top Field Trial dogs. If so, you are wrong. That would be like someone taking up motor racing and going straight into Formula 1. A purely field trial bred dog would, in most cases be too hot for a beginner and too fast and would have too much of a mind of its own – it would almost certainly be a couple of jumps ahead of its handler! Start with something a bit steadier from a dual-purpose kennel, of which a few still exist. Don't get me wrong; I'm not suggesting that because it is dual-purpose bred it will be a slouch, far from it, but my experience has been that, on the whole, these dogs are rather more tractable than others. So, whatever your requirement, look for the right kennel. How do you find it? Well, there are several ways.

1. Contact the Kennel Club (see Appendix 1). They will be able to give you the names and addresses of reliable breeders in your area.
2. There is a list of the various Golden Retriever Clubs in Appendix 3. Any of them will be only to pleased to help you.
3. Obtain, through your local newsagent, either or both of the national dog papers. They are *Our Dogs* and *Dog World*. Both are weekly publications in which breeders advertise.
4. Contact your local veterinary surgeons and ask if they can put you in touch with a reliable breeder.

5. Scan the pet column in your local paper and, indeed, the *Yellow Pages*, but be wary if more than one breed is being offered in the same advertisement; that could point to one of the establishments that I have already mentioned. A lot of genuine breeders advertise in their local press when they have puppies for sale and, indeed, many have advertisements in the *Yellow Pages*, but have a care.

Don't be surprised if, having found a breeder who comes up to requirements, they haven't a puppy available immediately – they can't keep puppies on a shelf and take down a suitable model when asked for one. Go and see the breeder and the dogs, have a good chat and, if you are happy after that, book one and be patient!

Capt: Dick Hermon, President, for many years of the AIGRC and breeder of the first Dual Champion 'Balcombe Boy' presenting a replica cup to the author for the Best Marker in an Open Stake in the '60s.

2

Commitment – Buying your Puppy

You have found a breeder whom you feel you can trust and who is prepared to be helpful. What next? First, ask to see the mother of the litter to make sure she has a good temperament, and has the loving kind nature and willingness to please which is so much part of a Golden Retriever's make-up. You may be able to see the sire, but often bitches are taken hundreds of miles to be mated to the most suitable dog. If satisfied, ask to see an up-to-date certificate for the dam of freedom from Hereditary Cataract and Progressive Retinal Atrophy. This should be from a recognised ophthalmologist, approved by the British Veterinary Association, more about this in chapter 16. Don't be fobbed off with anything like, "Oh they're fine; my vet looked at his/her eyes quite recently" The average veterinary practitioner does not have the equipment to carry out the required examination. If you are shown the dam's certificate only, ask to see a copy of the sire's as well – a competent and reliable breeder would have obtained one at the time of mating.

Assuming, however, that everything is in order regarding the eyes, enquire about whether the sire and dam have had their hips X-rayed and scored under the BVA/Kennel Club dysplasia scheme. At this stage the main things for you to know are that the hips are scored from 0 to 108 (54 for each hip), and that the lower the score the better the hip formation. In my opinion, and that of many other breeders, a higher score is acceptable in bitches than in dogs, but more about that later. However, having said this I put hip dysplasia about fourth or fifth on my list of priorities when selecting a puppy. One can have a dog with what appear on the X-ray to be diabolical hips and yet it never goes lame. Years ago I had a bitch, a superb mover with terrific drive, that won, amongst other awards, the Field Trial Class and Reserve Challenge Certificate at Crufts. Her main objective in life, as far as I was concerned, was work. Alas, she started to squeak, a cardinal sin at a field trial, so I decided to part with her. I had her hips X-rayed as there was someone from Sweden interested in her and in Sweden they were, and probably still are, hip mad. This was long before there was a

7

scoring scheme, but had there been one it would be my bet that she would have gone a long way towards 100! She eventually went to a wonderful home on a very large farm in Lincolnshire where she used to race around behind the Land Rover, jumping in over the tail-board when she'd had enough. She was regularly used for shooting until she was at least 11 and she lived for another two or three years after that – and she was never lame! When assessing the amount of attention to pay to hip dysplasia just think about this – freedom from hip dysplasia is not a major criterion in the breeding policy for the Guide Dogs for the Blind Association. Having said this, hip dysplasia is something to consider but, alas, even if one mates a dog with a hip score of 0 to a bitch with a similar score there is no guarantee that the progeny will have equally low scores. If hip scores are available, regard the facts as an added extra and note that the breeder is doing all that is possible to breed healthy, sound puppies.

Now, what is important is temperament. It is no good having a dog with a pair of clear eyes and perfect hips lying in front of the fire if every time you move you are snarled at or bitten. Possibly I am overstating the case a bit, but you'll get my drift. Fortunately, the vast majority of Goldens have the most wonderful temperaments, a fact which I think is summarised very well in a verse from a poem by the late Patrick Chalmers:

> The Golden Retriever I'd say for a start,
> Is as gold as a guinea in every part –
> Oh, he's golden of jacket and golden of heart.

It is their wonderful kind, intelligent and outgoing natures that has caused them to be in such demand as companion dogs for the disabled. These same loving characteristics have made them popular as PAT dogs, which visit old people's homes and hospitals.

Nothing, alas, in this world is perfect; there are exceptions, however rare. They are largely brought about by those ready to jump on the bandwagon and breed from anything, with a total disregard for basic requirements, including temperament.

However, you should already have checked on this when first visiting the breeder from whom you are hoping to get a puppy. By the way, don't go dressed in a city-slicker suit or a designer dress; the chances are that the dogs will quickly appreciate your desire to be friendly and will reciprocate. In spite of possibly being rebuked by their owner, they may well jump up. There are owners who will show you their dogs most willingly, but will not allow you to make a fuss of them or allow the dogs to demonstrate their appreciation of your visit. This, to a beginner, may seem unreasonable, but it is not, particularly if the dogs are used in the shooting field. The owner spends hours teaching them that he/she is the only person they must pay attention to, so the last thing that they want is their dog going up to all and sundry. As one very famous American trainer says in his book, when people visit him they don't expect to go and pet his wife, so why should they pet his dogs? So if you come across this situation, don't be put off, but note instead if tails are wagging and whether there is a soft and adoring look in the eyes that are firmly fixed on the boss. If you cannot resist the temptation, ask before you pat the dog, and if the answer is in the negative don't be offended.

So far, so good – what next? Ask to see an extended pedigree of the puppy. It probably won't mean a thing to you, but it sounds good to ask and you should learn something. Now, on most pedigrees, Champions are shown in red. 'Ch' before the name of a dog indicates that it is a full Champion. That means it has won three Challenge Certificates under three different judges at Championship shows and has either won a Field Trial award or has obtained a Show Gundog Working Certificate. 'Sh Ch' before the name means that the dog is a Show Champion and has no working qualification. 'Ir Ch' represents an Irish Champion, 'Ob Ch' Obedience Champion. 'FT Ch' indicates a Field Trial Champion, which means the dog has won two, or in some cases three, Open or All-Aged Stakes, one of which must have been for any variety of retriever. Not infrequently you may well find written under the names 'Eye Cert:' and a date and, to give a specific example, 'Hips 3–5' indicating a total hip score of 8. Don't be afraid to ask questions about the pedigree; any breeder worth his/her salt will only be too pleased to help. Indeed, some, if they think they've got a convert (particularly to showing) will, to coin a phrase, 'leave the donkey legless' with all their chat.

What else? It would be as well to enquire if the puppies will all be registered individually with the Kennel Club, or just as a litter. If the latter, then you will have to complete the registration if you want that done. However, the established breeder will almost certainly have registered each individual puppy, which will then carry the breeder's prefix. Then there is the question of choice. Many breeders give first pick to a customer who is looking for an eventual show or field trial dog. Others work strictly on the basis of first come, first served. Now, assuming you have your name down for a puppy, or have found a suitable breeder who already has puppies, it is well to enquire about how you stand regarding this so that there is no misunderstanding when the time comes to collect your pup. Most breeders will ask you to come and see the litter at around three to four weeks of age and, if you are satisfied, to pay a deposit then. I never consider a puppy booked until I have received a deposit.

The time has come to make your final selection, assuming that you have a choice and are not last on the list. What are you going to look for? Well, you want a good, healthy looking puppy for a start; if they look sickly and undernourished and have diarrhoea then you are at the wrong place! You are looking for a puppy with a good breadth of skull, reasonably pronounced stop and deep muzzle, and you should check that the bite is correct. That is, the top teeth should just protrude over the bottom ones – described as a good scissor bite. Look for ears of moderate size which are well set on, a good reach of neck and well-laid shoulders. You also want to see a short well-coupled body with a good spring of rib, a backside like an Aberdeen Angus bullock, a good turn of stifle and plenty of bone. The eyes should be dark, as should the pigmentation; that is, you want to see a black nose and pads. If you have any preference regarding colour, the ears are a good indicator of what colour the puppy will eventually be. One that looks cream but has dark ears will almost certainly finish up a deep rich gold by the time it has coated once or twice.

This all seems quite easy on paper but, to the untutored eye, it is not quite so easy in practice. If you have any doubts, find an experienced person to help you, perhaps the breeder from whom you are getting your puppy. All reputable breeders, and I make no apology for again using the adjective, are anxious to see dogs that they have bred do well. When finally making your selection at 7 to 8 weeks, ask, if it is at all possible, to see the litter running around in the garden or a paddock. This is particularly important if you have work in mind for your dog. Watch your choice. If it should appear more timid than the rest and try to get back to the kennel, I would be very inclined to forget it and look again, for the chances are that it will always remain timid and probably lack drive in the shooting field and animation in the show ring. Even as a pet it could grow up suspicious of strangers and generally rather nervy. I know there will be breeders who will not agree with me over this, but I can only go on what I have observed over fifty or so years. Having said this, I readily admit that there are always exceptions to everything and it is possible to develop both character and boldness in a timid puppy – but why take on more work?

Assuming your selection is into everything and shows a definite desire to explore, then approach it and see what reaction you get. If you are greeted with much wriggling and tail wagging, you're getting on. Now stand back from the puppy, clap your hands as loudly as you can and see what happens. Hopefully, the reaction will be one of interest and not fear. A partial retreat should be viewed with a certain amount of caution, so if that happens call all the other puppies towards you and try again. If you get no further reaction, fine. However if your choice heads the field back to the kennel, forget it, particularly if you are planning to work your dog.

Let us assume all is well. It is time now for the next move. Pick up the puppy of your choice, make a great fuss of it and, at the same time ask for the remainder to be put back in their kennel. When this has been done, squat or kneel down with the puppy, still making a great fuss of it, get out your handkerchief and tie two or three knots in it. Making sure that the puppy see it, toss it a short distance from you and watch what response you get. Hopefully the puppy will rush out and pick it up. Incidentally, position yourself between the retrieve and the line for the kennel. Even at such an early stage, instinct will tell the puppy, 'I've found something good, I'll take it home.' If all goes well, you can put out a hand and check the run for base. Having caught the puppy very gently, ease its mouth open and reclaim your handkerchief, or whatever soft thing you threw for it – it certainly will not hand it over at such a tender age. Making sure that the puppy is watching, throw the handkerchief just once more, a little bit further this time. If the puppy retrieves it, and having done it once it is almost certain to do so again, don't be worried if it runs off with it or makes a wide detour to pass you and heads for the kennel. That puppy's got brains. You took its new-found toy away from it last time; it's not going to get caught again if it can possibly avoid it. On the other hand, if it brings it straight to you, at that age that's a bonus.

Suppose the puppy won't retrieve; what then? Well, it is certainly worth having a few more tries, but if it hasn't an inherent instinct to pick something up there's not a lot you can do about it. Maybe you've heard or read somewhere about forced retrieving. Forget it; it certainly is not something for a beginner to try his/her hand at. You have two choices: either start all over again or take a chance that the puppy will have a change of heart when it grows older. It

Bryanstown Ingerid's (Bridie) puppies at 3$^1/_2$ weeks old.

really depends on what your chief interest is, but if it is work I'd think again.

Don't let's meet trouble halfway; let us assume all is well and that you have found a puppy that is pleasing to your eye, is not nervous and has an outgoing personality and a desire to retrieve. One small point: whilst handling the puppy you may have noticed that it appears to have dandruff. This will almost certainly be due to its being kept under infra-red lamp. If there are any signs of this, draw it to the attention of the breeder but, unless it is very bad, do not let it influence your decision.

By this time you should have been informed about when the puppy was wormed; if you haven't, just check on this one.

There are two final points. First, don't complete the purchase unless you are satisfied regarding all the foregoing. Remember *caveat emptor* – let the buyer beware – or, if you don't remember it, become acquainted with it. The chances are that in law, if something is wrong, it would apply. It is up to you to satisfy yourself that everything is in order. Secondly, I strongly advise that you take out an insurance policy from one of the companies specialising in pet cover* (see Appendix 4). Don't be alarmed; I'm not suggesting that you are going to spend the next ten to twelve years at the vet's. It is just a sensible precaution. Dogs, like humans, can become ill, but with them all medicine is private and, therefore, costly. With veterinary costs as they are today, insurance is something well worth considering. If you do not take out cover against veterinary fees, I do think you should make quite sure that you have third party cover. There was a case in the Eighties of which I forget all the details, but do remember that something in excess of £350,000 damages was awarded against a dog owner whose dog had been the cause of a multiple car crash.

That's it, then. The breeder wants a cheque, you want the Kennel Club Registration Certificate, an extended pedigree and, normally, a diet sheet. Incidentally don't get alarmed if the breeder cannot give you the Registration Certificate. The Kennel Club is not noted for speed in issuing these, although at last it seems to be improving. However, I do suggest that you get the breeder to write on the bottom of your receipted account 'Registration Certificate will be forwarded immediately it is received from the Kennel Club.' That keeps everything on a nice business footing.

Ch Willowlawn Lady Isolde, Winner of 4 CCs and 3 Res., bred and owned by Mr C. Ashton. Beginners should take careful note of this bitch if looking for a role model.

So, now you own a puppy and have, hopefully, committed yourself for a period that could reach up to thirteen or fourteen years, maybe longer. When you take the puppy home, I strongly suggest that it travels on someone's lap, lying on an old towel – it will feel more secure that way. Remember it is leaving the company of its brothers and sisters and, up to this time, it has never known that the world extended beyond the kennel and possibly the lawn. This is a big and frightening experience, but, equally, an exciting one. Close proximity to you will give the puppy confidence and start to cement the relationship which you are going to build over the coming months.

3

Early Days

So you're home; with luck the puppy won't have been too sick and if you're really lucky he won't have been sick at all! I think this is a good place to decide to refer to the puppy as 'he': 'it' sounds impersonal and 'he' is shorter to type than 'she'. As soon as you get him out of the car, give him a run in the garden, in the place where it is your intention that you will always take him to empty himself. When he has done what is necessary, praise him. It may sound daft to some to tell him he's a good boy for doing what come naturally, but it's the only way you've got of letting him know he's done the right thing.

If it's a nice day, let him have a scamper round before going into the house, but have a care – don't let him venture where he can come to harm. What harm? The answer to that is that there are quite a few things around the average householder's domain that could cause a pup to run into trouble. I will name just two. Not many years ago I sold a very bold outgoing puppy to some people who had a lovely house and grounds. It was in the spring and at the end of the garden they had planted some fruit trees between which had grown an abundance of stinging nettles. They were just coming through nicely, two to three inches high, a size, I have found, at which they appear to be particularly vicious. The pup went charging off into these, was most terribly stung and was very poorly for some days. People I knew as a boy had a wasp's nest in their garden; they were aware of its existence, yet they put their new puppy out unattended. It found the nest, went to investigate and was so badly stung that it was dead within a couple of hours. So, just make sure there are no hazards before giving your boy the run of the garden.

I have assumed, possibly wrongly, that you'll have everything ready for the arrival of the new member to the household. It has also been assumed, probably correctly, that he is going to live in, but there are exceptions. If it is your intention to kennel him, then his quarters should be ready. You will require a kennel at least 6 ft × 4 ft with a concrete floor; don't have a wooden one. A wooden floor would become impregnated with urine and stink however

Ch and Ir Ch Mandingo Buidhe Colum
(Sire Alresford Nice Fella, dam Buidhe Dearg)
BOB Crufts 1962. Winner of 7 CCs and 7 Green Stars. The first Irish-
bred dog to win Crufts
Owners Mrs W.H. Sawtell and Mrs E. Harkness. Breeder Miss L. Ross

much you scrubbed it. A raised wooden bed is essential, the kennel
should be well lit and ventilated, and ventilation should be
constructed so that it can be regulated. An outside run, at least
8 ft × 6 ft is a MUST if the dog is to spend most of its life in the
kennel. Ideally, the outer run should be covered and the whole
properly drained. If you buy a prefabricated wooden kennel, which
would be a great expense, spend a little more time and money and
line it with tin up to about 3 ft 6 in – it will be cheap in the long
run as kennel dogs can become very prone to chewing. Further,
when putting up the run, which will, presumably, be of chain-link
fencing, keep the wire on the inside of the uprights, that is, if they
are timber. That way you will avoid coming out one morning and
seeing the fence partially collapsed because the eager beaver, whom
perhaps you hadn't time to take for a walk the day before has
worked out his own mode of exercise and spent a happy night
gnawing through one of the posts. I kid you not; it can happen,
as I know from grim experience! If circumstances are such that
you have to kennel your dog, then a log of wood in the kennel

provides hours of entertainment and it is better that he should chew that than the kennel.

You will normally only get serious damage if your dog is bored but, of course, as in all things there are exceptions. I well remember one puppy I had, Tim. He was a super pup, very bright and almost over-affectionate. He was kennelled with two others around the same age. Apart from their spacious sleeping quarters, they had access to a very large concrete run. When he became old enough, Tim was doing an hour's road work a day, had a good gallop in the paddock every afternoon and, at the same time when he really started to make his presence felt, I was training him. He had a very full day! The first indication I had that he thought differently was when he started chewing up galvanised buckets – he treated them as though they were made of papier mâché! Then he started on the kennel, and tin was like chewing gum as far as he was concerned! I rebuilt the bottom part of the kennel three times, and no way could I catch Tim *in flagrante delicto*. I could see him hard

Ch Simon of Westley
(Sire Ch Camrose Fantango, dam Westley Frolic of Yelme)
Winner of 21 CCs, Five times winner of Crufts Gold Trophy for the best dual-purpose Golden, 4 Field Trial awards
Owner/Breeder Miss J. Gill

at work on his self-imposed demolition job from the bedroom window and would try to creep up on him, only to find him lying in the main run, looking as though butter would not melt in his mouth and very pleased that I'd called to see him! All the while he was growing and growing; by the time he had laid waste to the kennel for the fourth time, he was well over the breed standard height. This, plus his insatiable desire to chew, sealed his fate: Tim had to go.

I telephoned a professional trainer I knew well and explained the situation. No problem, *his* kennels were indestructible and he would be pleased to take Tim until between us we could find him a good home as a gundog. I had a phone call about a week after Tim had moved; he was getting on well but, the trainer was sorry to say, his kennels were not indestructible! About six weeks later Tim was sold to what sounded like a super home and I learned that he was to live indoors as a shooting companion. I was horrified to learn that the house was full of valuable antiques! Some weeks passed before I plucked up courage to telephone and enquire how he had settled down. Absolutely wonderfully, I was told; he was in fact the greatest thing since sliced bread! I took a deep breath and nonchalantly enquired, 'No problems with chewing or anything like that?' 'Chewing? Good gracious, no. Whatever gave you such an idea?' Oh well, I thought . . . I . . .' My powers of speech failed me. 'Don't worry about him; he sleeps on the end of our bed and no money could buy him from us.'

I'm glad to be able to add that he turned out to be an above-average gundog. There is a point to this story. We have for decades bred for temperament, which includes love and affection. There are dogs that really crave human companionship – Tim was one.

To return to junior, he must have a place of his own if he is to live in – an anchorage. I would suggest that you make him a wooden box, approximately 3 ft 9 in × 2 ft 9 in and 2 ft 3 in to 2 ft 6 in high with boards that will drop into slots in the front so that, during the early days, you can shut him away for a while if you wish. If you screw the side boards in place, when he grows up you can remove these down to a height of 8 in to 9 in and then he will have a bed for life. Of course, you can buy plastic or wicker ones, but you cannot shut your youngster back into one of these and the latter are particularly attractive for him to cut his teeth on! Preferably, his bed should be placed where there is a tiled floor or something of that nature so that he can run around at night; you don't want to force him to dirty his bed. As far as bedding is concerned, to begin with I suggest a bit of old blanket, or at least something that is of no value so that it won't matter if it gets ripped up.

House-training should commence at once. There is absolutely nothing to be gained by putting it off and allowing bad habits to develop. The sooner you start, the sooner you will have a puppy that is clean in the house and, with a Golden, that shouldn't be long; they are simplicity itself to train in this regard. So, as I have already said, when you get home give him a run in the garden before going into the house. When you take him indoors, let him explore, but PLEASE don't let all the family try to fuss him at once; everything will be very new and strange to him. Whilst he's sussing out his new surroundings, keep a watchful eye on him. If you think he is about to squat, grab him quickly, but quietly, and take him outside to his place. Put him down and encourage him with whatever words you decide to use. I always say, 'Good boy [or girl], hurry up.' When they get older, for me it is a matter of putting them out of the door and saying, 'Hurry-up'. From my wife it's 'Pish-wish'. Both commands have the same effect, which doesn't mean that our dogs are bilingual, just that they have an association of a given sound with a certain act, but more about that later. If your puppy does have an accident in the house, don't scold him unless you catch him in the act. If you do, grab him quickly, very firmly say 'No' and rush him outside, but don't make too major an issue of it. After all, you are the teacher, as such it is up to you to forestall such a happening until he knows better. Stay out with him until the mission is accomplished then give praise and take him back to the house. Yes, it's all a bit of a bore, but it will be well worth a few weeks' effort. Try to develop a routine, which is really repetition, the basis of all early training. When your puppy wakes up, and I'm talking about the first month or six weeks that you have him, take him out immediately. Do the same as soon as he's had a meal and, indeed, at any time when he seems restless. Of course, to begin with, he won't go through the night. If at all possible, let him have the run of the room where his box is and put down paper by the door, he'll quickly get the idea. It is probable that he will be 14 to 16 weeks old before you start coming down to a clean floor. A lot depends on the time you go to bed and get up in the morning; certainly he will not be able to contain himself for eight or nine hours.

As I have already said, you should have received a diet sheet when you collected your puppy. It could be that for a number of reasons this may not be suitable for you, particularly from the point of view of obtaining supplies. However, as far as possible, keep to the feeding that the puppy has been receiving, at least until he's settled into his new environment. Find out from the breeder what milk powder has been used and try and keep to it. Cow's milk is not concentrated enough. Without going into any great detail, cow's milk contains about 3.8 per cent fat and 13 per cent solids, whereas a bitch's milk has around 9.5 per cent fat and 24.5 per cent solids. There are numerous milk powders available for puppies, but for years I have used, with great success, a calf milk powder and mixed it in a higher concentration than that recommended for a calf. It is excellent and much cheaper than the powders sold for puppies. The only problem for the owner of one puppy is that you will almost certainly have to buy a 20 kg bag, far more than you will need.

Feeding is largely a matter of preference. There is a wide variety of excellent foods available these days. For many years I have used Skinners Puppy Meal, with very lightly cooked mince mixed with it. But it really is a matter of choice; however, at an early age changes should be gradual. By 8 weeks of age your puppy should be taking about 4 oz meal and 1 to 1½ oz mince twice a day. By meal I mean a complete food; strictly speaking, it is not necessary to give anything else with this but the addition of some meat makes it more palatable. I give this at 8.00 a.m. and 4.00 p.m. At 12.00 noon and again between 9.00 p.m. and 10.00 p.m. each puppy gets a half pint of full cream milk, that is, milk made up from a powder. These quantities are purely guidelines and as the puppy grows they must be increased. One essential for good feeding, be it for a race-horse, a bullock being prepared for the Smithfield Fatstock Show or your puppy, is a clean feeding bowl. If your puppy's motions are loose, then you are feeding him too much, so cut back a little. If he is loose to the extent of having diarrhoea, then cut out one or two feeds completely until he is normal, and give him something to tighten him up. A hard-boiled egg often helps. I would advise any dog owner to always have available a small supply of suitable anti-diarrhoea tablets, obtainable from your vet. There are also a number of proprietary remedies available from pet shops and chemists for the same purpose.

At 12 to 14 weeks I stop the midday milk feed. Entirely depending on the puppy, I continue the evening milk for as long as it is accepted up to 6 or even 7 months of age. Frequently a puppy will wean itself off milk before then. Feeding, on the whole, is a matter of common sense. Don't overfeed but, during the first year of his life, your puppy wants all he can take without growing too fat or having an upset tummy. Once a puppy has finished growing, he will require less food, about $1\frac{1}{2}$ lb meat and the same of biscuit per day, or 1 to 2 lb of a complete food; it entirely depends on the individual. Water should ALWAYS be on hand, particularly when feeding a complete food. There is masses of literature available on feeding, so no more space need be given to the subject here. However, before moving on, I will give one word of warning: don't be too lavish with the meat, that is, the protein. That can lead to problems. As a horse will get above himself on too many oats, so will a dog that is fed excessive protein. I have come across several examples of this.

The first example was a $4\frac{1}{2}$-year-old Golden Retriever I met when I had a boarding kennel. In plain language, he was an absolute sod. His owners were terrified of him as, indeed, were most of my staff. He suffered from chronic skin trouble and would most certainly bite the hand that fed him! Fortunately, we never seemed to have the pleasure of his company for more than a weekend. Then the time came when he was booked in for about six weeks, whilst his owners visited a son in Australia. When Rusty, who was most aptly named, arrived he was in a foul mood – he'd bitten his boss that morning! In addition, he was covered in raw patches, a form of eczema which the vet had assured me was not infectious – he looked a mess! The owners had collected some lotion from their vet, but they were too scared of their pet to apply it, for every time they tried he flew at them. Before they left, the owners handed me an envelope. I enquired what it was and was told it was written authorisation to have Rusty put down if we could not manage him. To this day, I don't know what prompted me to enquire what they fed him.

'Oh 2 to 3 lb of raw meat a day' was the answer.

'No biscuit or brown bread?'

'No, he prefers meat.' Then, with a giggle, 'We always hope it will stop him biting us!'

I began to warm towards Rusty; perhaps he wasn't such a bad boy after all. When the owners had departed, with not a tear in their eyes, I decided it was time Rusty learned a few facts of life. It was quite a struggle and he bit through two old ties before his mouth was securely tied up. I admit I was not too gentle, but I had his death warrant in my pocket and I did not want to use it! By the time I and my kennelman had cleaned up his skin and dressed it, he was a much chastened dog. He received no food that day and was put on to a diet of Luda biscuit and cooked tripe from then on. The result was quite miraculous. Within seventy-two hours he was a different dog, his skin problem started to clear up and by the end of a week one could pat him without being even growled at, never mind bitten. After two weeks he was everybody's friend and, at the end of the six weeks, I returned a fit and happy dog to his owners. They couldn't believe he was the same animal they had owned for a number of years. Fortunately, they took my advice on feeding and Rusty lived as a much-loved and devoted pet to a ripe old age. I have applied the same principle on several other occasions with equal success.

What to me was common-sense feeding has been thoroughly researched and developed by Dr Roger Mugford a consultant on animal behaviour. The following are observations and recommendations made by Dr Mugford, who is always willing to assist owners who have a problem that may be related to feeding.

A Low Protein Diet for Dogs

Diet can play a role in some behavioural problems in dogs. Some dogs are incapable of metabolizing a high protein diet – or a diet containing poor quality protein, in particular some Golden Retrievers.

The diet outlined below is designed to test whether the problem behaviour is related to diet. It proves some 15–18 per cent protein calories compared to a level of 30–50 per cent found in most commercial or prepared pet foods.

We are aiming for a good quality, easily metabolized protein source which is balanced for your dog's requirements. That is why we recommend lightly-cooked meals rather than diets exposed to intensive cooking or over-processing.

If diet is a relevant factor in your pet's behaviour, then it should be apparent in 2–3 days. We would advise that you use this diet for 7–10 days. Please contact us at the end of that time to report progress. If there is an insignificant improvement in behaviour, we would then recommend that you use a low protein compounded diet.

The Rice–Mutton Diet

1. Boiled chicken/mutton/fish/rabbit.
2. Boiled white/brown rice.
3. A vitamin/mineral supplement – Stress or SA37 or Canovel (use as directed on the packet).

4. Vegetable oil or sunflower oil or corn oil
    (1 tablespoon/10 kgm body weight).

Mix the meat and rice in the proportions of 4 parts of boiled rice and 1 part meat. Feed the usual quantity of food.

It may be worthwhile varying the type of meat used to give variety to the diet. Mashed potatoes can be substituted for the rice.

From the earliest days, you must make it abundantly clear that you can take anything from your puppy at any time that you wish. I always make a point of stroking puppies whilst they are feeding, then taking the bowl away and returning it. Even one small growl gets an instantaneous response – a quick slap and the command 'NO'. Should you receive an adverse reaction to your training, a couple of these lessons should ensure no further trouble. If you don't nip such behaviour in the bud, you are building up problems for yourself in the future. I have come across numerous cases, in all breeds, where owners have let a possessive streak develop and the faint-hearted have finished up with their dog dictating where they can go and what they can do around the house. Sadly, such cases usually finish up with the dog being put down and it is usually the fault of the owner for not having brought the puppy up correctly. Rules of behaviour should also apply to such things as getting off chairs, should you allow your puppy to get on them in the first place. Personally I do not think an armchair is the place for a gundog, but it's up to you. I remember one evening, at a friend's house, where we all sat on hard wooden chairs whilst the Goldens were allowed to occupy the settee and armchairs! After a long and tiring journey I found this, to say the least, a bit off.

You should keep your puppy away from other dogs and you should never taken him out on the streets until he has had his jabs. This will be at 12 and 14 weeks, and they should give him an immunity from distemper, leptospirosis, hepatitis and parvo virus. Your vet may well suggest a second parvo shot at around 16 weeks. The reason for this, in the simplest terms, is that your puppy will have received parvo antibodies from his mother. At 12 weeks these could still be at such a level that they will nullify the injection given at that time. Unfortunately, the immunity that the puppy received from the bitch is not long lasting and a second jab is advisable. You are probably wondering why you should vaccinate against parvo virus at 12 weeks. The answer is relatively simple;

research has shown that the cover provided by the bitch may only last for 7 or 8 weeks, which is one of the reasons for virtually quarantining him until he has had all his shots.

You will receive differing advice on future booster injections from various vets. All are agreed that it should be an annual event but some like to cover a wider spectrum than others. Many years ago, before the advent of parvo virus, I took the counsel of a very eminent veterinary surgeon and on his advice, I had our dogs fully boosted every third year and annually against leptospirosis. The latter is particularly important if you live in the country and take your dog along by a river or stream. The commonest source of infection is rats and just after a flood, when the rat holes in the banks have been washed out, seems to be a particularly dangerous time.

You must be guided by your vet regarding parvo virus, and indeed for all forms of immunisation. However, for reasons I will not go into now, some two to three years after parvo had raised its ugly head, I had all our dogs, who had been annually innoculated against parvo, blood-tested and checked for their immunity against it. All had, according to the pathologist, a life-long immunity. This I found interesting and it does give one food for thought regarding annual boosters.

Get your puppy out in the car as soon as possible after he has been vaccinated. The quicker he learns not to fear it and gets used to it, the easier life is going to be for you both. To begin with, make the journeys short and if the ride leads to a field, or somewhere which is fun, so much the better. He will quickly associate the two. Should you have an estate car or hatch-back, where the puppy will be behind a dog guard, then plenty of newspaper is the thing to have. It's such fun to tear up, it keeps his mind off other things and it does save the matting if he's sick!

There is one very simple rule regarding exercise up to 6 months: no long enforced walks. Free running in the garden, a park, a field or wherever you can let him off for a gallop is fine, but let him set the pace. None of this being led along the road for two or three miles. Why not? The answer is simple: as the puppy grows, so, obviously, do his bones; new cells are being formed all the time. These bone cells are soft to begin with, so excessive exercise could cause damage. As an eminent orthopaedic surgeon once said to me, 'People are quite extraordinary. They would never dream of making a 2$\frac{1}{2}$- to 3-year-old child walk two or three miles. Yet they consider they have been clever in making a puppy do so.' I well remember a man to whom I had sold a puppy ringing up one night and being really offensive. The puppy, who was about 5 months old, was lame. I enquired where. From the garbled reply, I gathered that he was intermittently lame all round. The abuse and rudeness continued and my fuse was getting very short! He stopped for breath, and at last I was able to get a word in. 'You know what the trouble is; you haven't been giving him enough exercise.' He took the bait. 'Of course I have; he's been doing at least two miles every day, whatever the weather, ever since he was fully vaccinated. What sort of a fool do you think I am?' I told him!

I always make a point of getting a lead on a puppy as soon as possible, at 10 weeks or even less; not a collar, just a slip lead – that is, a straight cord or piece of webbing with a ring at the end, so one can make a noose, similar to a choke-chain. It is most important to put this on correctly, so that it will slacken immediately if there is no pressure on the lead. This means if you start with the lead without a loop in the end, standing on the right of your dog and bringing the ring in the end of the lead round under the dog's neck from the left and passing the end of the lead through the ring as you bring it up on the right. If you put it on in the reverse way when pulled up tight, it will remain right.

When you first put a lead on your puppy he will resent it strongly and pull and cavort to the limits of his leash. Talk to him and quietly coax him, even drop the lead and let him pull it around for a few minutes. He'll quickly learn and will soon give up fighting, but don't try to do it all at once. It will take about a week, but don't spend more than ten minutes a day on this, that will be quite enough – remember you want to come out of these training sessions still friends! Once he has reached a stage when he is not fighting the lead and has had his jabs, take him to some place where he can watch traffic, not too much to start with. Traffic can be awesome enough to us at times and we know what it is. Think how you'd feel if you had never seen a vast articulated lorry and, suddenly, there was one charging at you up the road. If you can find a bank to sit on, or open space, back a bit from the road, so much the better; let him see two or three vehicles and then call it a day. Increase the time slowly and it should not be many weeks before he ceases to worry very much. I have found that once you start walking on the road to begin with when you hear a large or, indeed, fast vehicle approaching, it pays to turn and face it. Around 5 months of age you can start short road walks – three or four hundred yards – and slowly build up from this until, by the time he is a year old, you are doing between one and two miles a day.

One final point on the subject of exercise: from about 5 months onwards, when out for a stroll, if he wants to hunt you should not only let him but encourage him. The bolder he is and the more he'll enter cover, the better.

It is important, from the earliest days, that a puppy should become used to being groomed and by the time he is 8 weeks old a brush and comb should not be strange to him. Even five minutes a day will suffice, providing it is done regularly. From the start make it clear that this is not a game, and that he must stand up and be still. Of course, this will take time, but keep lifting him back on to his legs saying 'Stand' every time he sits down or rolls on his back. You'll be surprised how quickly he'll get the idea. There are a variety of grooming tools available, but basically a comb, brush and, possibly, a grooming glove are all you need, the former being by far the most important. You can obtain these from any reasonable pet shop and they should be able to advise you. Should you have any problems, contact Messrs Allbrooks Ltd (see Appendix 1). If you do not groom regularly and, indeed, properly, your puppy's coat will start getting matted. It was not unusual to have long-haired dogs coming into the boarding kennels I used to keep whose owners were adamant that they groomed their pets every day; however, I would find great mats behind and below the ears, behind the elbows and inside the hind legs. To get rid of these, straight and thinning scissors are needed and they are costly – it's cheaper and much nicer for your dog to groom him diligently every day for five or ten minutes.

When grooming, keep an eye open for any unwanted visitors, that is, fleas. The first indication of such a visitation that you will probably have is the presence of flea dirt, little black pieces of matter (flea excreta) about the size of a pin-head. However careful you are, sooner or later your dog will pick up the odd flea, particularly if you live in the country. Treatment is simple; there are numerous remedies available from pet shops and chemists. However, I have found Nuvan Top to be the best and the easiest to use. It comes in an aerosol and a quick spray the full length of the back should do the trick. If you decide to use this you will almost certainly have to get it through your vet, although some chemists do now stock it.

One particular thing whilst grooming: always check the ears to make sure they are clean. This is very much an area where a stitch in time saves nine. Ears can be the very devil to get right if you have a deep-seated infection. A useful thing to keep by you for cleaning these is Dermisol Multicleanse Solution – again, I'm afraid, you will have to get this from your vet.

Finally, under this heading, there is drying. If your pup gets very wet, towel him off when you come in, indeed, do this when he is older as well. The great thing is to get his back dry, especially across the loins. Towels are the obvious things to use; some people use a chamois leather; and, in an emergency, newspaper makes an excellent substitute for more conventional methods as it is amazingly absorbent.

Make sure nails are always kept short. With plenty of road work, normally they will not need cutting. However, if they do, DON'T try cutting them with ordinary scissors – you'll split the nail. Buy a pair of nail clippers – I prefer the guillotine type. Be careful not to cut back beyond the quick; in case you do, it is handy to have a small jar of potasium permanganate crystals at hand; when applied these will quickly stop any bleeding. If your nerve fails you, take your dog along to your vet or to any dog beautician – but don't let the nails become too long before you get around to doing this.

Here is a tip that may be useful, before moving on. If you get tar on your dog, and this is quite common when road repairs are being carried out or when a heat-wave causes the road surface to melt, it will come off quite easily if you rub butter on it and then wash the area. Unsalted butter is best but any will do.

In the days of my youth, teething was an anxious time; that is, when your puppy is from 4 to 5 months of age, losing his milk teeth and gaining his permanent ones. In those far-off days, feeding was inadequate and often caused a calcium deficiency. That frequently led to puppy or teething fits; these could quite often be fatal. Today such fits are almost unheard of. However, it is important to examine your puppy's mouth two or three times a week at this time. It is not at all unusual for the permanent teeth to start coming through before the puppy teeth have dropped out. This can lead to the puppy, temporarily, having a double row of teeth. If you see this happening and the milk teeth seem quite firm, it would be as well to get your vet to have a look and take out any that may cause trouble. When examining the puppy's mouth, be very quiet and gentle. If you hurt him he may well start to object to people taking a look and that may eventually lead to his backing away from a judge in the show ring – the judge has to check that a dog has the correct bite, which is as was mentioned in the previous chapter.

Right, that's the basics out of the way. Now, a couple of pointers as to how you can subtly work in a little painless training. Get yourself a sensible whistle, that is either a Staghorn or an Acme with or without a pea – the pea these days is usually cork. I say 'sensible' as there are whistles available and sold for use with gundogs that are ideal for starting a swimming race or calling the police, but really make the welkin ring when used in the shooting field! Equally, don't go to the other extreme and get a silent whistle. Those who advocate the use of these have never tried to handle a dog hunting in a field of sugar-beet on a windy day! I use two Acmes: one without a pea as a stop whistle and one with a pea for the recall. I will go into the question of the use of the whistle in more detail later; at this stage all you want to know about is the recall. That is 'pip pip pip' – three quick, short notes. Now, during these early days, that is up to 8 or 9 months, you can train your puppy to come to the whistle by using it to call him back in every time you put him out in the garden. After calling him by name, immediately give a quick 'pip pip pip' on the whistle. The sequence is, name, whistle, name, whistle, until he comes. Of course, to begin with he won't have a clue about what is going on, but, providing you make a fuss of him every time he comes to you, he'll soon put two and two together and come to the whistle alone. Plenty of fussing but NO tidbits; if you start the latter you are building up problems for the future.

Mr & Mrs McDonald Wood's Ch Revelsgold Sargeant Pepper. A quality dog with 3 BOBs, 5CCs and 8 Res CCs to his credit.

The other thing you can get is a PUPPY dummy. No, it's not something to suck; it's a dummy for retrieving, some 6 or 7in long, canvas covered and with a soft filling. Both this and the whistle you should be able to get from a gunsmith or even from some pet shops. If you have a problem in getting what you want, contact Turner Richards (see Appendix 1). Providing your puppy will bring the dummy to you, give him the odd retrieve when you are out for a walk. Obviously, he must see you throw it. ALWAYS make sure you are between him and home, or him and the car if you have gone off for a drive. If he picks the dummy up but will not bring it to you, forget it for the time being. If he will, one retrieve, or at the most two, on a walk should be enough; in fact, it is enough. This will mean it is fun and a treat for him. Whatever you do, never let him run off with it and start chewing it. Should this happen, get after him at once, take the dummy from him and don't let him have the dummy again until serious training commences. When this starts it must be old-fashioned schooling; none of this modern nonsense of being brought up with no repressions. Your boy is in for quite a few repressions if you want him to grow up into a sensible, nice and useful test or shooting dog!

4

A Preface to Work

James Lamb Free, one of America's most famous gundog trainers, writes in his book, 'No matter what you have heard or read to the contrary, there isn't so much to training a good retriever. There's nothing to it that a fairly bright moron couldn't figure out for himself.'

I'm not sure that I entirely go along with the above, but there is a modicum of truth in this statement. One of the most profound remarks I ever heard on the subject of training a gundog was made to me by an Irish friend, who said, 'You want plenty of time when you're training but not a lot of it.' Sounds Irish, doesn't it? But what it boils down to is a little and often. It is no good having a marathon session one day and then doing nothing for a week! Ten to fifteen minutes is quite enough during the early stages of training. If I were asked what were the greatest and commonest mistakes made by a beginner I would, without hesitation, reply, 'Trying to do too much too quickly.' But I do not go along with the school of thought that says you must only teach one thing at a time. If you embark along that road, both you and your dog will be grey before he's ready to be taken out on a day's shooting! Another appalling mistake made by beginners is chastising a pupil for some error when he has come back to them. By chastising I mean even the use of a hard tone of voice, never mind a good shake or even a walloping! You have got to go out to him and stop whatever he's doing when he makes an error. It may be that you will find out how fit you are as a result and you'll puff and blow a bit, particularly if you have a really keen, hard-going young dog, but it's got to be done. It is no good trying to straighten him out when he's done what he's been taught, that is, has come back to you when you whistled or called him. If you berate him then, well, I'd certainly classify you as one of Lamb Free's morons! Your puppy will think he's in trouble for doing what he thought was right and for doing something that, in the past, you have praised him for.

Let's stop and consider what training is. To reduce the definition to its most basic terminology, it is, quite simply, imposing your will upon your dog in such a way that he enjoys it – nothing more, nothing less. Actually, if you have done what has already been suggested, you are already a trainer, albeit only an apprentice one; hopefully, he doesn't piddle in the house any more, because you have willed him not to. He walks on a lead – all right, he may still pull at this stage, but he doesn't fight it; this again is because it is your will that he should do so. I well remember calling one summer afternoon many years ago on my good friend Eric Baldwin, one of the most talented and knowledgeable trainers I have ever met. Having got no reply when I rang the doorbell, I made my way around the side of the house, heading for the kennels. There I came across Eric weeding a flower-bed.

'Hello, I didn't expect to find you gardening', I greeted him.

'Well, I'm not really. Just filling in time whilst training.'

I must have looked a bit blank. Eric indicated left and right and there lying on the lawn at either end of the long border was a dog.

'They have to learn that if I say "Sit", be it for an hour, ten minutes or whatever, that is what they do. If you are going to have a top trial dog it has to be 100 per cent yours, and enjoy being yours.' He looked at his watch. 'That'll do.' He called up the Golden to his left. If I remember correctly, it was Palgrave Volvo, later to become one of the great Field Champions of the breed. Volly knew school was over and rushed to his owner. The adoration was plain to see. Then, having been duly praised, he immediately sat on command whilst the other dog, a Labrador, was called up. The second dog showed the same exuberance as the Golden. We walked off to the kennels, both dogs tight at heel.

'How long were you there?' I asked.

'Oh, about an hour to an hour and a half.' I looked at the two dogs – they were full of bounce. There was no question of their being cowed. That's the hallmark of a good trainer – an obedient, happy dog.

The time has come to consider what your minimum require-ments are for training, for without the tools you cannot do the job. It will be assumed that you already have a whistle; if not, get one. You shouldn't attempt to start training until you have one. A choke-chain is most essential. A medium-weight one will do. You don't normally need one with ¼ to 1 inch links, as appear to be used in training police dogs; if you do, as a beginner, you are way out of your league. I would suggest you have a minimum of four dummies. The best ones are canvas covered with plastic sealed interiors, weighing about 1 lb, are 11 to 12in in length and are fitted with a throwing toggle, (Turner Richards* see Appendix 1). There are other makes available, and you can, in fact, easily make your own. Actually a home-made one, of the right sort, can be very useful.

Get an empty washing-up liquid soap container or something similar, 10 to 12in long and fill it from a third to half-full with sand. If you haven't any sand around, buy a packet of bird sand from a pet shop! Cover the container with an old sock and sew up the end. Don't, as I have seen done, knot the end by so doing, leaving three or four inches of the sock after the knot; if you do, nine times out of ten a puppy will get hold of that instead of picking up the dummy properly. I usually tuck the surplus SOCK back inside before sewing up and completing the dummy. Now, the clever thing about this dummy is that it helps your puppy to learn how to balance a retrieve. If he picks it up at one end the sand runs to the opposite one and makes it more difficult to carry. He will soon discover that if he picks it up across the middle it is easier and he doesn't get his feet and legs tangled up with it.

Right, you've a whistle, a choke-chain and dummies; what else? You need about thirty to forty yards of light nylon cord, and I do mean light: one-eighth to three-sixteenths of an inch will be quite heavy enough. An old tennis racket and some equally old tennis balls are a great adjunct and will most definitely be required in due course. A couple of feathered wings will be needed as the training advances. These can be bought from Turner Richards, but frankly I don't recommend those they sell, simply because they are white. By the time you require the wings, your puppy should be getting his head down and using his nose. If the wings are white, I have found that a puppy starts to look rather than hunt for them. If he can see them, the chances are that you can as well – remember that you want a dog to collect game that you can't see! If you can see it, then, in all probability, you will be able to pick it up yourself. You require your dog to retrieve what you cannot see and to do that he must use his nose and hunt. I find pheasant wings ideal for introducing a puppy to feathers. You can get them from a poulterer or maybe you have a friend who shoots who will be able to help you. If you happen to live in the country near a big shoot, there's a very fair chance that you'll find a dead pheasant that's been hit by a car on the road. Take the wings off at the end of the first joint from the body. With a sharp knife, cut away as much of the little meat there is and rub in alum, then lay them for about ten days to dry. If you do this, they'll last for years. Finally, a blank cartridge pistol that uses .22 blanks should complete your immediate requirements as far as equipment is concerned. There is a lot more that you can get but, at this stage, don't require.

This is as good a place as any to say that before you start training, for goodness sake practise throwing a dummy. The number of beginners I have seen whose efforts in this sphere can only be described as pathetic is considerable. Nearly always they let go too late, and the dummy flies up into the air and lands about five yards away! I actually once saw one hit the thrower on the top of the head; he had no idea where the dummy had gone! So take your dummies, go off on your own, find a bit of open ground where you'll see them when they fall, and practise. It's really quite simple. Hold the dummy by the toggle, and the cord between your first and second fingers. When the dummy is straight down by your side, that is 0°; when your arm is straight up in the air, that is 180°. Bring the dummy back behind you to get some impetus going, then swing it forward and release it when your arm is at an angle of 60–70°. The action is more of a flick than a full-blooded throw and you should be able to get the dummy out a good thirty-five to forty yards. It is very worthwhile to train yourself before you start training your puppy.

Now for some do's and dont's. To start with, let's get rid of a very common myth. Your puppy doesn't understand, in the way that we understand, every word you say. You may argue that when you say 'Walkies', he knows and rushes to the door. If you said 'Dictionary' every time before taking him for a walk, his reaction would be the same! The best example of this I ever came across was a lurcher, owned by a poacher who was a perfect menace for a while on the estate where I grew up. The poacher had trained this bitch, Rose, totally in reverse. For example, 'Come here' meant 'Get out' and vice versa. When the owner was caught poaching by one of the gamekeepers and was told to call his dog in, the more he shouted 'Rose, come here', the harder she went for home! It was quite a while before the keepers worked this one out.

Accept that your dog does not understand the meaning of the words you use, he merely learns to relate a certain sound with a certain action that is required of him. A dog has no reasoning power; he relies entirely on his memory and, believe me, that can become very good indeed. So, as you train your puppy, you must develop this. Some, like humans, have better memories than others. It has been my experience that the dog that appears to be ultra-intelligent simply has a better memory, and it is almost a certainty that such a dog has a greater love and interest in what is going on and what he is being taught than most.

When you start training, you have to assess how good your puppy's memory is and note how quickly it works. How do you develop it? By repetition; it's just as simple as that. There is a word of warning, however: particularly during the kindergarten stage, don't be repetitive to the extent of becoming boring – remember that the secret of good training is a little and often. Always stop when an exercise has been done well and your pupil is keen for more. PLEASE only use one command for one exercise. What that command is doesn't really matter, the choice is yours, but having decided, stick to it. I recently saw a puppy in a working test. It had a lot of potential which, alas, could not be said for the handler, who sent the young bitch for an unseen retrieve. She was launched with a series of high-pitched 'Hi lost's – one would have done, for the puppy was gone on the first command! She worked nicely, but she was short of the dummy, and eventually she stopped and looked at her handler for help. A quiet 'Go back' and the appropriate signal would, I feel fairly certain, have produced the desired result but, alas, that was not to be. Admittedly the handler was very nervous. The commands came thick and fast – 'Go on', with no reaction; 'Seek', again with no reaction; 'Oh do go back, you stupid dog' – and so it went on, until the handler was told to call her dog in. The latter had stood, apparently mesmerised by the cacophony of sound being aimed at her, waiting for a command that she could relate to some exercise she had been taught. I talked to the owner after the test. She assured me that the bitch, worked marvellously at home and went back without any problem. I enquired what command she used. 'Why, I just say "Get back" and signal accordingly.' She was somewhat surprised when I told her that, of the many exhortations she had tried to get her bitch out to the retrieve, she had failed to use the only one she claimed her dog understood!

Once you are quite sure that your puppy understands a command, never give it without enforcing it, but be certain that its meaning is truly stored away in his memory. If you are sure that he knows it and he does not carry out your command, then he's cocking a snook at you. Let him get away with this and it will not be long before he ignores you again and then again. If you let this happen you might just as well stay at home and watch the box, because he will have learned that he need not do what you say and will have, for all intents and purposes, terminated your training efforts.

It is very important, in the early stages, to do your training in complete privacy. You don't need the help of the kids, nor mother-in-law standing by and making such helpful remarks as, 'That's not what it says in the book.' Let's face it – it's all new to you and the puppy. Try to find a fairly confined space to start your training. If you have a large garden, much of the initial work can be done within its confines. Whatever you do, don't start trying to train your puppy in the middle of a large field or common, where there are bound to be things to distract his attention; he might even ignore you and go off for a good gallop. You have to command his full attention. That's one reason for keeping the sessions short. After ten minutes or so, he'll lose his concentration – just like you used to do sometimes at school! I know I am repeating myself: it is intentional. Do all your initial training in privacy until such time as his work means more to him than anything else; neither you nor he requires spectators to distract you from what you are doing.

It does seem incredibly difficult to get this point about privacy across to a beginner. I well remember the Eastern Counties Golden Retriever Club arranging a talk and demonstration for beginners at Eric Baldwin's. Eric and I gave a demonstration of handling and he then gave the most excellent talk on basic training. It was a gorgeous day and he gave the talk in his paddock. On a table he had laid out the tools of the trade, which included a dozen or fifteen dummies. Throughout his talk, Eric kept reiterating how essential it was to be on one's own when training and that there must be no distractions. He finished his talk by saying, 'Well, I think that is all you can absorb for now; remember, a little and often on your own.' He paused, turned and winked at me and continued, 'If any of you want to use the dummies you may.' There was a rush and in seconds the table was cleared. Dummies were soon flying in all directions, a dozen or more whistles were sounding, there was shouting, running and jumping about – it seemed as though the field had been suddenly invaded by Morris Dancers. Half a dozen or so of the audience remained by the table. One turned to Eric and said, 'Thank you, Mr Baldwin, but I don't know why you waste your time!' I hope I have made my point!

Finally, as I have previously said, during the time leading up to the start of training, let your puppy run and hunt anywhere you can, particularly in cover. Give him plenty of freedom, get him used to going across rough country, jumping ditches and generally finding things out for himself. I am, of course, assuming that you have reached the stage at which he will come to you when you call, or, if you have done what I suggested, when you blow a whistle. When he's running loose don't check him; if you do, you'll only make a rod for your own back because when you want him to go out and hunt he'll think he has to stay at your heel. Anyone can stop a dog. I have yet to meet anyone who can make one go without a great deal of work and, even then, it is seldom successful. Just so there is no misunderstanding, having a good gallop doesn't end when you start training. When school is over it should be time for play, but from this stage onwards it is you who will decide when it is playtime. Even when fully trained, your dog, like you, wants to be able to relax. When you do let him run free, right from the start, give a command such as 'Get on' so that later he will know that it is in order to gallop around.

5

Problems and Discipline

So far, the assumption has been that your pup will pick up and carry, but what if he doesn't? You can't embark on training a retriever if the silly animal will not retrieve! If this is the case, what can be done? Many people would say there is not a lot and that if he hasn't the natural instinct to retrieve, he's not worth bothering with anyway. In most cases this could be true, but there are always exceptions, and if you are keen to turn your pet into a working gundog all possible avenues should be explored. It is, of course, entirely possible these days that the show purists will have bred out all working instinct, albeit unintentionally, in their search for beauty. However, the natural desire to work takes a lot of killing; if you have a puppy whose pedigree is full of Show Champions, there is a chance, be it ever so small, that the desire to work is there but dormant. Fortunately, I have only encountered two or three dogs that would not pick up and retrieve – I hasten to add that they were not of my breeding – but in all cases I eventually managed to get them working.

Let's assume you have thrown a dummy on the lawn, or somewhere where he can see it, and that he has run to it but will not pick it up. Pick up the dummy and tease him with it, that is, wave it around his face. Try to get him excited and encourage him to take hold of it. If he does, praise him, let him hold it and, if he will, let him walk about with it. If this happens you are more than halfway there and the chances are that, after a few days of playing with the dummy, he will run and pick it up when you throw it; but don't be in a hurry. Keep teasing him with it and letting him take it out of your hand, until it has become a game that he really enjoys. When you think he's really keen and has the dummy in his mouth, take it from him and, making sure he sees it, throw it for him. It is almost a certainty that he'll pick it up and run off with it. Don't let the latter worry you as long as he doesn't start to chew it. If he attempts to do that you must get to him and quietly take it away from him. Although it is a major crime, don't scold him. Even if he wants it, don't let him have the dummy any more that day.

If you have carried out my suggestions, you should have a nylon cord. Attach this to a collar or to his lead and let him trail it around until he gets used to it so that he will still consider himself to be free. When you have achieved this, you are ready for another try. However, before going into action there are three things to attend to. First, see that the line is either coiled or laid out in such a way that it will run out freely. Secondly, make sure you have a good stout glove on the hand you are using for holding the cord, for if he picks up the dummy when you eventually throw it and makes off with it at any sort of gallop, when he gets to the end it could easily cut you to the bone! I know; I made the mistake of not using a glove when checking a very good bitch I had that started running in. She was brought up smartly, having launched herself at full gallop, after about forty yards. We both learned a lesson – she never ran in again and I never used a check-cord without a glove. Oh, by the way, for the uninitiated, running in is going for a retrieve without being sent. Now, thirdly for goodness sake don't throw the dummy farther than the length of your line. Nothing could be more off-putting, once his enthusiasm has been aroused and he has been sent for the dummy, then to be brought up short before he reaches it.

He's attached to the cord; play with him as before, taking the dummy and throwing it. At this stage, make absolutely no attempt to keep him from running in; let him chase off as you throw it. As he picks it up, start calling or whistling him back to you. If he runs off, keep your voice soft; don't let him get the idea that you are displeased with him. You shouldn't be. What you are doing is getting him to pick up a dummy; everything else at this stage is secondary. Now apply the brake, but try not to stop him with too much of a jolt, the gentler the better. To achieve this you may have to move forward behind him. When he has stopped, call him and gently haul him in. When he's back with you, make a great fuss of him and let him hold the dummy for a few moments if he wants to before taking it from him. You can repeat the exercise once more before calling it a day – remember, a little and often! Within a matter of days he should be coming back to you without your having to reel him in. However, even when he does pick up the dummy and heads straight back to you, let him trail a length of nylon for a while, until it becomes automatic for him to retrieve to hand.

What if he doesn't respond to teasing him with the dummy? Well, it's a case of trial and error. Throw a ball for him, a piece of stick, an old sock, anything, but try to find something he likes and will pick up.

If you can achieve this, then, whilst it may be a hard slog, you should be able to get him retrieving. Obviously, once he's started to pick up, the remarks about using a check-cord apply whatever it may be that he has decided he likes. I was once given a 15-months-old yellow Labrador dog. He had a nice personality, would hunt and loved the gun, but in no way would he retrieve. I was desperate until I noticed that he had a bone to which he was particularly attached. I took him out on to the lawn and threw it for him; he raced out and picked it up and trotted off with it. I tried again with the same result. I attached him to a cord and the next time I was able to get him back to me, plus bone. In due course I put the bone in an old sock. After some hesitation he eventually retrieved it. From then on he never looked back.

You can try putting the dummy in your dog's mouth and getting him to hold it. This can work but, more often than not, he will fight you and try to spit it out. However, if he does hold it and will start to carry it, then you proceed in the same way as you would if you had persuaded him to take the dummy whilst teasing him with it. Another thing you can try, instead of a dummy, is a dumb-bell. A very famous American trainer, Charles Morgan, claims to have had good results using one; he says that because the bar is raised off the ground a dog can pick it up more easily than a dummy. Actually it's not a bad thing to try putting in your dog's mouth – it's not as bulky to hold as a standard-sized dummy.

If you haven't had any success so far, we're beginning to run out of options; but there are a couple of things you can still try. A dog will often retrieve from water, providing, of course, that he likes swimming. To begin with I would try with a bit of stick, again because it is easier for him to get hold of than a dummy. There are several IFs that now come into play. If he will enter water and if he will grab a bit of stick, you must meet him at the water's edge to take it from him; don't let him put it down if you can possibly help it. He'll probably shake himself all over you, but don't make a fuss about that – it's all part of the job! As you repeat this amusement, slowly move back from the water's edge but ensuring that he brings his retrieve to you. Then when you are a few yards back, toss your retrieve in on the edge of the water, so that he doesn't have to swim. If this works, keep moving back and if all goes well eventually throw the dummy just short of the water and pray! Many years ago I bought a golden bitch about 20 months old. She would do everything except retrieve but, eventually, after hours and hours of patient work, I got her going as I have just described above. In her case what was particularly annoying was that whilst I was trying to get her to retrieve, her litter brother had won a Novice Field Trial; he later went on to many more successes in the field.

Now we come to my last suggestion. If your puppy is sufficiently interested to run out to a dummy or ball when you throw one, is delighted to find it but won't pick it up, then the following might work, but it means getting some help. You want to find someone who has a dog that will retrieve and who is prepared to lend a hand. Again, this is something I have tried and it has worked. Throw the dummy and send your puppy for it; when he's found it, send an older, experienced dog who will grab the dummy away from under the puppy's nose. Then throw it again and send both dogs together. The old dog will get the dummy and the youngster may well try to take it from the opposition, which is not usually a good thing but at this time it is a plus – he's getting jealous! Then throw it again, but don't send the experienced dog until the pup is nearly at the dummy. Your youngster will hear him coming and grab the dummy – we hope. If he's not sufficiently jealous and just stands back as if saying 'be my guest', then, I'm afraid, there is nothing more I can suggest, except getting another puppy and starting again. If, however, the ploy works, I strongly suggest that you take the trained dog along for a number of sessions, just to keep your pup feeling 'if I don't get it, he will'.

Now we come to the really thin ice, nearly always skated around or totally ignored in books on training; it is the question of punishment. Yes, I'm talking about a good shaking or even a walloping when your dog has done something wrong. When he deliberately ignores a command that you know is safely stored away in his memory, he is just showing contempt for your authority and, if you want to continue training, you have got to take a firm stand. No, I'm not a sadist; I love my dogs just as much as you, possibly more, but I have no desire that they should become undisciplined hooligans and a menace to those who come in contact with them, like so many members of the human race. Remember that your dog doesn't reason, he doesn't think things through, so you cannot appeal to his better nature, and he is not going to learn wisdom with age and grow out of his teenage stupidity. You have to find a way of getting it across to him that he has done wrong. Further, he will remember the punishment, whatever you mete out to him, as being connected with what he was doing at the time you administered it. So NEVER, NEVER call your dog to you and then discipline him for something he was doing before you called him to you. I know I am repeating myself, but if you do that he's going to think he's getting into trouble for doing what he has been taught to do – coming to you when called. If you are stupid enough to do this, you'll very quickly find that your dog becomes very shy of returning to you. If he does wrong when out working, you've got to get your running shoes on and get out to him – catch him in the act!

Fortunately most Goldens are pretty sensitive when compared with Labradors and flatcoats and, frequently verbal chastising will be sufficient. If that is not enough, a good shake, or even possibly a walloping with a rolled-up newspaper, is all that will be needed to deter your pupil from committing the same crime again, but remember that he doesn't reason. Let's take an example. You are well on with your training and your dog knows what the recall on the whistle means, but he ignores it. You get out after him, catch him and give him a good shake, blowing the recall at him, then put him on the lead and, not too gently, yank him back to where you were, still blowing the recall at him. He will remember your displeasure as being about one specific thing – ignoring the recall whistle. Now let's assume that you are sufficiently far advanced in your training for him to know what the stop whistle means, but he ignores it. When he does this, he doesn't stop to think, 'Hang on, I was in trouble the other day; I might be again today if I don't pay attention'; the two situations are two totally unconnected matters as far as your lad is concerned. So you've got to stir your stumps, get after him and go through the whole boring business again; alas, it's the only way he'll learn.

Now, having said this, if you've done your job as a trainer correctly, the chances are that you may never have to do more than a little verbal admonishment, but you've got to face up to the fact that more may be necessary, particularly if you have a really keen, hard-going dog. In his book, which must be considered a classic on dog training, James Lamb Free devotes a chapter to this subject, entitled 'Spare the rod', and I will quote one paragraph:

If your dog ever demands a showdown apply only as much pressure as needed to win the argument and command obedience. There are dogs so sensitive that a disgusted look and harsh words are sufficient to do the job. This is not true of most retrievers. When it has become plain that you must deal out punishment, do it. But remember that every form of canine punishment is effective less by virtue of the pain it causes than by revelation of the power of the administrator. If it does not instil in the dog an appreciation of the power of the trainer to impose his will, it has missed its mark – and has probably thrown the training program backward.

Incidentally, when Lamb Free refers to retrievers, he means all breeds, for later he goes on to say, 'But the rolled-up newspaper makes quite a startling noise, and one good application often gets amazing results, even with a Labrador or Chesapeake – and is likely to be all that will ever be needed with a Golden.'

As I have already implied, most Goldens are very conscious of a harsh tone of voice; this coupled with a good shake – that is, catch the dog by the loose skin at the side of the neck just behind the head with both hands, lift his front legs off the ground and simply shake him – should normally do the trick. If not, a walloping with a rolled-up newspaper may be required. As Lamb Free says, it is noisy. It is also an indication of your extreme displeasure, but it is in no way hurtful. If you don't believe me and want to check, wallop your leg with a rolled-up paper, remembering that your dog's skin is a good deal tougher than yours and that he has a nice thick coat acting as a buffer!

As a beginner, if you cannot get results with what I have suggested, then I think you want some professional help and it might be well worth your while to consider sending your miscreant hound to a trainer to be straightened out. It all depends on how serious you are over this training and on the nature of the crime. There are times, contrary to what many readers will think, when a real thrashing is warranted, and taking a long-term view, is very much to the advantage of the dog concerned. I have been involved in two such cases. Once, about forty years ago, I was out riding with a lady. Her Golden was accompanying us, and suddenly he dived through the hedge and there was an awful commotion. He had grabbed a sheep! Realising what had happened, I leaped off my horse, pushed through the hedge and literally seized the dog by his tail, pulling him off the sheep, and laid into him with a hunting crop that I was fortunately carrying. The speed and severity of my attack did the trick; he never looked at a sheep again. As virtually every dog owner knows, sheep worrying is the most heinous of crimes and a farmer is, by law, entitled to shoot a dog caught doing this. Alternatively, if a dog is traced after worrying and the owner is taken to court, it is almost certain that there will be an order made to put the dog down. The other time involved a Golden bitch that was to be put down if no one would take her. I took her. She was, according to her owner, totally uncontrollable and an avid chicken-killer, and she had been the cause of much expense

Ir Ch Bryanstown Diplomat of Ulvin (Sire Ch Weyland Varley, dam Ch Charming of Ulvin) Retrieving his first shot bird. Winner of 15 Green Stars, 9 Field Trial awards.
Owners Mr and Mrs M. F. Twist. Breeder Mrs L. Ulyatt

to her owner. She was only 16 months old and, from a work point of view, bred in the purple. I quickly found that her claim to fame was not exaggerated. There were two courses open. One was deliberately to let her perpetrate her usual crime, so as to catch her in the act, and really straighten her out. The other was to carry out the sentence already virtually passed on her. I chose the former, and it worked. She trained on to be an absolutely super gundog and lived to be nearly 14 years of age – preferable, I feel, to being put down at 16 months! Having said this I am very much against beating dogs and, particularly in the case of Goldens, it should not be necessary; but, as in most things, there can be exceptions, as I think I have more than illustrated.

6

The Basic Rudiments of Work

The time has come seriously to start training and to test your patience, of which, incidentally, you'll probably require a great deal before you've finished. It has to be assumed at this stage that your pup will pick up a dummy and that, if there were problems in this sphere, they have already been ironed out. Further, it is assumed that he will, at least most of the time, come immediately you call or whistle him, preferably the latter. To recall your dog, use a quick 'pip pip pip' on the whistle and to stop him or make him sit use a short, sharp blast. Remember this; don't just blow in an aimless fashion on your whistle; he will learn to understand this form of communication even better than words of command. You will find that the really top Field Trial handlers virtually never use their voices when handling a dog and they limit the use of a whistle to the minimum; when they do use their voices you can be sure they are having problems! It must also be taken for granted at this stage that your puppy will lead.

Now serious training commences. When school is taking place, junior graduates to a choke- or check-chain, instead of a slip lead. A word of warning; never go through a training session with a collar on your dog, except possibly when using a check-cord. To leave a collar on your dog is to expose him to possible danger when working in cover or jumping fences. He could get hung up and choke to death before you could get to him. Always make sure that the choke-chain is put on correctly so that it slacks off immediately there is no pressure on it, in exactly the same way as the slip lead you have been using does.

The first thing to achieve is to get your pup to walk at heel on a loose lead. What exactly does that mean? Before elaborating on this, are you left- or right-handed? You'll probably wonder what that has got to do with it. I'll tell you. The reason the majority of people train a gundog is because they shoot and to shoot you must carry a gun. If you are right-handed, then you will normally carry the gun under your right arm, therefore you want to train your dog to walk on your left. That way you will avoid the possibility of frequently banging him on the head with the end of the barrels or, even worse, shooting him! The chances of the latter happening are pretty remote, but I do remember a boy walking through a wood with a gamekeeper who had an old-fashioned hammer-gun under his arm; the gun was cocked. Whether a twig caught the trigger or something went wrong with the mechanism I don't know, but, whatever the reason, the gun went off and literally blew the head off his spaniel, which was walking just under the end of the barrels. Play safe and train your dog to walk on the opposite side to that on which you would carry a gun. Having decided this, the next thing to establish is the correct place for a dog to be when at heel. For me, it is on my left side, his shoulder level with my knee, so that he has a view of at least 180°. Why should this be necessary? The answer is, so that he can mark, that is, see, the fall of anything shot or, if you are into working tests, see dummies thrown out in front. It is part of his job to see and memorise where things fall. I remember once judging at a Field Trial and being paired with another judge, also of many years' experience. We were in sugar-beet when one of the country's top handlers came into the line under us. Off we went and immediately the dog tucked itself in behind the handler's knees – it could see nothing. This did not please me or my co-judge who, after we had gone some thirty or forty yards, turned to the handler and said, 'Get your dog up alongside you so that he can mark.' 'That's all right, sir' came the reply. 'I'll mark and he'll fetch.'

But it wasn't all right! He had what should have been two straight forward marks, out in front of the line. In both cases, the dog had to be handled on to them. For those who don't know what handling means, it is stopping one's dog on the whistle and then by hand signals directing him to the retrieve. A properly positioned dog would have seen both falls and should have been able to go straight to them without any assistance. In this particular case the bad positioning cost the handler any further participation in the trial!

I will assume that you are right-handed, but should you not be then, of course, the following will need to be reversed. Start off with your pup on your left, holding the lead in your right hand, about waist high. I normally keep my left hand lightly resting on the lead as well. As you move forward give the command 'Heel'. If he pulls ahead give a sharp jerk on the lead with your left hand and repeat the command in a crisp tone of voice. Do not keep a continuous pressure on the lead, so that you develop something akin to a tug-of-war. Quick sharp jerks are the things to use with a check-chain. Continue these, plus repeated commands, until he is walking beside you and has ceased to pull. The lead should be quite slack. If he starts to move out from your side, slap your left hand on your thigh and jerk him back so as to keep him up to you. Do not encourage him to look up at you by talking to him. Most of you will have seen obedience trained dogs on television or at shows walking gaily along, literally touching the handler's leg and looking up at his/her face. You don't want that; first, because your dog wants to look ahead so that, later, he can mark the fall of any game shot; secondly, when walking a field of sugar-beet, potatoes or any root crop sown in drills, your dog has got to be in the next row to you, not tight up to your leg – there won't be room for the two of you in one row! Further you don't want your dog so close that there is even the remotest chance that he could trip you up when you are carrying a loaded gun.

Normally there is little trouble in teaching a dog to heel, but you will get the odd one who tries to hang back. This, normally, is for one of two reasons: either he is a bit apprehensive of what is going on, or he is being subjected to more control than he has been used to in the past and is being a bit sulky about it. There is another possibility, namely, that you have been too tough on him and he has become wary of you. Whatever you do, don't try to drag him along. All that leads to is his fighting against you. Try a sharp jerk on the lead; if he comes up to the required position, slacken the lead at once and give him plenty of praise. This is one case where tidbits are permissible. I have found that a bit of cooked liver in my left hand will normally brighten up the most persistent laggard, but normally I am not in favour of bribery!

You may find that you have a persistent puller. Normally a series of sharp jerks on the choke-chain and the command 'Heel' will solve this problem. I did have a dog years ago that just did not seem to get the message, so I armed myself with a garden bamboo cane, about 3ft 6in long, took the lead in my left hand and swung the cane, like a pendulum, in front of the dog's nose. This worked for a couple of days, but then he decided he could push past the cane. However, a few sharp raps on the nose soon disillusioned him over this and it was not long before he was walking correctly at heel.

Right, your boy now walks at heel in the correct position on a loose lead. The next thing is to get him walking at heel off the lead. If you have done your lead work correctly and are not in too great a hurry, this should be no real problem. I suggest you slip the choke-chain off and just lay it across his neck. He thinks you still have control, which of course you haven't, but it has the desired effect. I was given this tip, by a gamekeeper more than sixty years ago when training my first gundog on the estate where I grew up. He described it as the dog 'being tied up loose', which really is a most apt description. Then, as you are walking along, gently lift the chain off and, normally, all will be well. If he is inclined to stray lay the chain across his neck again, give the command 'Heel' and slap your leg. Unless he is ultra-dim he will quickly get the idea that 'Heel' means heel, whether he is on a lead or not.

Earlier I said that I was not of the school that thinks only one lesson can be taught at a time. While you are teaching your puppy to heel you can introduce other essential basics such as sitting, short-marked retrieves, sit and stay and run-backs. I normally start off with teaching walking at heel, sitting and a marked (or if you prefer, seen) retrieve. I also make as much use of the whistle as possible; this I will explain in a moment. When your puppy starts to get the idea about walking at heel on a loose lead, introduce the next element – sitting. If you have read any books on training you may, particularly in older ones, have found that the command suggested is 'Hup' – presumably a derivation of 'Sit up'. However, I prefer 'Sit'. It is a crisper command and, when a dog becomes advanced in his training, if he is straying from heel a quiet 'Sssss' – like a hiss – will bring him back to your side. Similarly, if he is becoming restless at a pheasant drive when sitting, a quick 'Sssss' may well settle him down and remind him that he has got to remain where you have dropped him.

To make your dog sit, give the command 'Sit' and, at the same time, an upward jerk on the lead. With the other hand, press down on his hindquarters until he is in a sitting position. Start to do this at intervals as you are teaching him to heel. He should sit on command after having been put into the sit position eight or ten times at the most. From then on, a light upward jerk on the lead and the command 'Sit' should produce the desired result. If it doesn't, you've just got to persevere with pushing him down. Maybe he's a slow starter, or maybe you've got yourself a dumbo; if the latter, you've a lot of work ahead of you and you'll need a lot of patience. There are dogs, fortunately very few, who seem to have no memory. I was once asked by a very great friend, a well-known breeder of Goldens, if I could help her get her Qualifying Certificate – now called a Show Gundog Working Certificate – with her dog; they had already won a Challenge Certificate, but were just getting nowhere on the work side. I said I would and had the dog to stay. To say that he was thick as two planks would have been an understatement. He loved the gun, so there was no problem there, but when one took him out every morning he had totally forgotten everything that had been done the previous day, so it was back to square one every time. After a month the only command he'd assimilated was 'Sit', but once he had sat it was one heck of a job to get him to move! He would pick up a dummy with great gusto and run off with it. A check-cord was no help, because he didn't seem to be able to remember its effect from day to day. After a month I sent him home as untrainable. A few months later he was sent to one of the top professional trainers; he threw in the towel after just three weeks.

Let us revert to training your pup to sit. When he is doing it without any bother in response to a quiet command, start giving a short sharp blast on your whistle immediately following the order 'Sit'. You will find very quickly that you will be able to dispense with any verbal instruction. In doing this you are starting to make him whistle conscious, an all-important factor for the future. Before you have reached this stage, you can finish off your training session by throwing a dummy for him a couple of times, making sure he sees what you are doing. Make him sit, off the lead. The chances are that if he's really keen he'll be nearly underneath it, mouth open as it lands but, at this stage, don't worry about that; he's keen and that's what you want. Now I shouldn't have to remind you about what follows, but I will. Make sure you are between him and base when he picks up the dummy. Base may be home, the road for home or your car, in which you have brought him out to your training ground. In these early days there could still be a tendency towards 'finders keepers'; if there is, he will head for what he considers to be a safe sanctuary. If you have taken the precaution advised and he starts to run off with the dummy, DON'T RUN AFTER HIM – he'll think that's a great game! Instead, head towards base, calling or whistling him; if he's reached a stage where there's any semblance of obedience, he'll follow. When he catches up with you, stop, turn and take the dummy from him – but quietly, don't snatch at it. If you have to grab anything, grab him, not the dummy; you don't want him suddenly locking on to it as that's the way to develop a hard mouth! When you have the dummy back in your possession, praise him. That retrieve, for him, has given a nice fun ending to the lesson. If he ran off with the dummy and you found dog training to be a rather more athletic pastime than you had anticipated, remember to take and use the check-cord the next time and the next until he is coming back to you without hesitation.

At this juncture, I will add a few words on the subjects of hard mouth and failing to give up a retrieve. The two are not the same. Hard mouth is biting or, quite literally, compressing a retrieve.

This, of course, normally does not show up on a dummy, but it is very evident with game or rabbits. However, it does not mean that a dog will necessarily tear the flesh. What usually happens is that a hard-mouthed dog picks a bird or rabbit across the back and exerts so much pressure that the ribs are crushed. When he comes to hand, in all probability he will give it up without any bother. It is, however, an eliminating fault in a field trial and something to be watched for and guarded against from the earliest days of training. Frequently a hard mouth is the product of bad training. Snatching or pulling at dummies can be fatal, so, later, can hitting a dog who persistently runs in when he comes back with game. His keenness is such that being inadequately trained, he breaks and, in a moment of euphoria, picks the bird. Then, on his return, he remembers from past experience that he's going to get beaten and, quite literally, grits his teeth in fear. This is a typical example of what can happen through the stupidity of chastising a dog when he comes back to you!

Now those who try to hang on to a retrieve are quite a different kettle of fish. It's just a case of, 'I've found it and I want to keep it!' That is not a good idea, and it is one that needs to be discouraged right from the start. When it happens, take hold of the end of the dummy with one hand and, behind the dummy, slip your thumb in over the bottom lip and press down on his teeth, at the same time giving the command, 'Dead'. If you do this hard enough it will nearly always work. It will not be long before you've only got to touch his bottom lip and he'll give up the dummy. There are several other alternatives, but only two need concern you. Shove a finger in behind the dummy and press down the back of the tongue to make him gag; he will spit out the dummy automatically. This has one possible drawback – he might close his mouth before you get your finger out! The other option, of which I don't really approve, is pinching the ear really hard between thumb and finger-nail. However, I did resort to this once, having nearly lost a finger when training a Labrador belonging to a friend of mine who had run into a number of problems. He was a keen dog and learned quickly. It wasn't long before I had only to touch his ear and he gave up the retrieve at once. I told the owner to do this when I returned his dog, but not why. I think he thought I had strange training methods, but he carried out the instructions and never had any problems.

When you think the command 'Sit' is fully retained in your pup's memory, take things a step further, to sit and stay. This means that you want him to sit whilst you walk away. Now, if you think you are going to just say 'Sit' and happily walk off, and he'll remain where he is, you're wrong. What you've been doing has been to make him sit when you have stopped whilst doing heel training. Now you have to teach him to stay. Have him on a lead, that is, on the choke-chain attached to a lead, give the command 'Sit', turn and face him. Holding up one hand, take a step back, repeating the command 'Sit'. If he moves, IMMEDIATELY put him back where he was and push him down with sufficient force for him to know that you aren't pleased and, of course, continue to tell him to sit. Then try again. You may have to put him back half a dozen times before he'll sit long enough for you to get the length of the lead away. When this happens, keep him sitting for a few moments before calling him to you. Repeat the exercise a couple of times and then call it a day for that session. Go through the same drill each training period from then on. It shouldn't be long before you can leave the lead off and go eight or ten steps away from him. Gradually increase the distance, but be watchful. Once you are certain he knows what he is meant to do, if he breaks and runs to you before he's called put the choke-chain on and, with some good quick jerks on it, take him back to where he should be sitting and put him down again with a really stern 'Sit'.

Sometimes a dog will be very obdurate over doing this. When I come across one like that I bring the check-cord into play. Pass it around a fencing post or small tree, having first laid it out in a straight line on the ground. Then sit the dog as close to the post as possible, attach the cord to the end of the lead, pick up the cord and, keeping a steady pressure on it, move backwards, giving the command 'Sit'. The moment he tries to move, give a hard jerk on the cord, at the same time repeating your instructions. You may have to go forward a few times to sit him down again, but keep the tension on the cord. When you have moved back a few yards, still keeping the cord tight, go back to him and tell him what a great chap he is! Repeat this for as long as it takes him not to move over a number of training sessions. When he makes no attempt to move and you can get to the end of the cord, drop it and call him to you. Incidentally, make sure there is nothing that the cord can get caught up on – you don't want to check him when you do eventually call him. The next thing is to sit him in the same place, still attached to the cord, but don't put it around the post – it's the old tied-up loose situation again! He believes you are still in control, even though you are not. Finally go through the routine in the same place, but without the cord. If all goes well, that's another lesson packed away in the memory bank. However, should he start to forget, don't mess around; run out to meet him, put the choke-chain on and really drag him back to where you told him to sit, berating him as you go. Remember, when he disobeys an order once you are sure he knows what it means, he is virtually challenging your authority. Let him know that 'Sit' means sit until you tell him otherwise, for the rest of his days.

Your repertoire of exercises is increasing, and as it does things are becoming more interesting for your pupil. That's a thing you must watch right from the start – maintaining his interest. If you think he's not paying attention and getting bored with proceedings, immediately call it a day, but always try to finish on a high note with something he will enjoy, such as a marked retrieve or a run-back.

This introduces the next element in training. What is a run-back? Exactly what it says. When you are finishing off a training session, put your puppy on the lead, let him see you drop a dummy and then walk off towards base. He'll keep looking back, wanting to retrieve it. As soon as he seems to be forgetting it, stop, slip him off the lead and give the command, 'Go back'. Ninety-nine times out of a hundred the puppy will rush back for the dummy. Incidentally, leave it in the open where he can quite easily see it. If he fails to go for it, then you've gone too far; he's forgotten it. Start again and slip him off the lead whilst he is still anxious to get the dummy. When he has got the idea start increasing the distance until you are sending him back fifty to sixty yards. I always end training sessions with a run-back, once a puppy knows what it's all about.

Mrs Daphne Philpott with Ft Ch Abnalls Hilary of Standardwick. For many years until her death she was a partner in Miss Joan Gill's famous dual purpose WESTLEY kennel. They shared the two prefixes, made up 21 champions on the bench and bred and owned many field trial winners. Daphne was one of a small group of Judges being both an 'A' panel field trial judge and an International championship show judge.

7

Intermediary Training

The basics having been satisfactorily instilled into your pupil, you are now reaching the stage when the more difficult elements of your undertaking have to be tackled. However, before moving on to these, let's give a little thought to two essentials in the repertoire of any worthwhile gundog – the ability to jump and to swim.

Much depends on circumstances and your enthusiasm for what you are doing when you decide how to start to develop his athleticism over a fence. If you are able to make a jumping lane, then it becomes a comparatively simple task, so let's begin with the easy option. To make a lane you will need some twenty to twenty-five metres of wire-netting, which should be at least a metre high. Erect this about a metre away from and parallel to a solid fence, one your puppy cannot push through. The wire-netting must be firm and taut so that he can neither push it down or force a way out underneath. As far as the obstacles are concerned, you can, to a degree, let your imagination run riot. Mrs Wentworth-Smith, owner of the famous 'of Yelme' Kennel and past president of the Golden Retriever Club for many years, had a lane that was akin to a show-jumping course! That sort of thing is all good fun but not truly necessary. I would suggest three jumps. The first one I usually make with some light branches, bound together with a few strands of wire – like an old-fashioned faggot – making a jump of some 15 to 18 in Make up several faggots of different dimensions, so that you can increase the height of the jump as your pupil becomes more proficient. For the second jump, set four uprights, two either side of the lane, about ¾ in apart, so that you can slot some lengths of old board in and build a fence to the required height. I do mean old boards, for there is absolutely no point in buying expensive new timber. Most builders will have odd lengths of old planking or off-cuts, destined for firewood, that will be quite suitable for your requirements. The third fence should be wire-netting, the commonest obstacle that you will find in the shooting field. However, do not try your lad over this until he is clearing the other obstacles with ease. When you feel the time is right, fix some netting across the lane. The easiest way I have found to do this is to thread a length of plain wire, about ⅛ in in diameter, along the top and you can then attach this to the sides of the lane. I normally tack the bottom to a piece of wood and roll some of the netting round this to start with, unrolling it to increase the height of the jump as required. Now all you need is some form of temporary gate at either end and you are ready to go.

Take the puppy in and close the gate. Toss an old tennis-ball over the faggot, give the command 'Over' and encourage him to fetch it. At a height of around eighteen inches this should be no problem to him. You may be wondering why a ball and not a dummy. The answer is that he can get the ball in his mouth and it will not impede him as much as carrying a dummy. If he is successful, throw the ball over the second fence, having previously fixed the jump at the required height, again giving the command 'Over', and send him over the two obstacles. Ninety-nine puppies out of a hundred will think this is all great fun but, as in all elements of training, don't be in too big a hurry, and don't over-face him. When he is flying over the fences, dispense with the ball and start using a dummy. Incidentally, when your dog is nearly fully trained and jumping well, not only in the lane, but also over other obstacles as well, start him retrieving heavier dummies, eventually working up to ones weighing 3 to 3½ lb. Like other dummies, you can buy these, but I make them by using an empty liquid soap container or something of that nature. Fill it with sand to the required weight; if it is still not heavy enough, take out some of the sand and add a few old bolts or pieces of iron, put the container in a sock and there you are! There will be those who will not have grasped the significance of using a heavier dummy. It is simple; a cock pheasant can weigh up to 3½ to 4 lb. For an experienced dog this is quite a weight to retrieve over a rabbit fence (wire-netting to keep rabbits out of a young plantation or away from a crop) or similar obstacle. A little practice in bringing back such a weight could stand both you and your dog in good stead in a field trial or, indeed, on a day's shooting.

If you cannot or do not want to make a lane, then you will have to call upon your resourcefulness. This will mean obstacles at exists from the house or kennel, at the garden gate and any other place where you regularly go and construct a jump. Once he learns, you will find your lad really enjoys jumping. I have had a number of dogs who, during play time would race off over a couple of jumps, coming back obviously pleased with themselves and almost saying, 'Gosh, I'm clever.'

Now what about swimming? You should start this when it is warm, not in cold, frosty weather. NEVER throw a reluctant puppy

The author with (from l to r) Ir Ch Bryanstown Shannon of Yeo, Ch and Ir Ch Bryanstown Gale Warning, Ir Ch Bryanstown Camrose Gail. (Not in their 'show clothes' – photo taken at the end of a day's shooting). All Open Stake winners and a total of 33 field awards between them.

in. The best way to start is to find a pond or slow running stream with a good hard bottom. Put on a pair of waders or change into your swimming trunks and walk in, encouraging your puppy to go with you. Have him on a lead by all means, but don't drag him in. Play with him with a dummy in shallow water, making a game of it. When he has overcome any apprehension he may have shown, throw the dummy parallel to the shore so he can race after it, still in shallow water. When he's retrieved this a few times and is obviously enjoying himself – they're like kids, the majority love splashing about in water – throw it so he has to JUST go out of his depth. Before he knows it, he'll be swimming. Then it is a case of yet again hastening slowly and giving him time to develop his new-found prowess. If you run into problems and have a friend with an older, experienced dog get him to join you. Frequently a puppy will follow such a companion. However, be careful and confine your activities to close to the shore to start with.

Should this not work, there are a few other things that you can try. Find a stream that you can wade across, but which is deep enough to ensure that your puppy has to swim, even if it is only for a few feet, if he follows you. Take your lad down to the edge. If he will not go in, you go on over, calling him all the time. When you are across, keep going, whistle him and keep walking until, if necessary, you are out of sight. There is a very good chance, once this happens, that he will literally take the plunge and join you. Just a word of caution; if you are going out of sight of your puppy, have someone he knows waiting at the car or, if you have walked from home, waiting on the return route, in case he decides not to follow but to go home instead. There is no point in taking unnecessary risks!

If the above strategy fails, you've really little left except physically putting him into water so that he has to swim. You have two choices. First, wade in, carrying him, to a depth when he'll have to swim when you put him in the water. Don't just drop him; ease him in, keeping his head above water. You don't want to scare him more than is necessary. Further, let him into the water facing the shore. When he reaches terra firma, fuss him and let him know how pleased you are. Try him with a dummy in the shallows. If he goes after this, fine; you've nearly won. If he's not interested, take him out again and let him swim back to land again. Once he finds out he's not going to sink he'll quickly get over his nervousness. Your second choice is really a variation on the first, the difference being that you launch him from a boat. I strongly suggest that you do this over the stern, for unless your boat is very stable, if you try putting him in over the side the chances are that you'll both be swimming! Make sure if you do this that you are close to the shore.

Incidentally I'm not in favour of starting a puppy swimming in the sea, although I know several people who do. The puppy nearly always drinks quite a lot of water when swimming and salt water could make him sick and put him off. These two necessary attributes, jumping and swimming, can be developed slowly from very early days, that is around 5 to 6 months.

Now to what, so far, is probably the most crucial part of his training – steadiness to a seen retrieve. That means he has to remain sitting until he is sent. Up to this stage, this has not mattered and he may well have been halfway to the dummy by the time it hit the ground. He has, I hope, rushed out and raced back with the dummy; in fact, with luck, he's become a retrieving psycho! Now you have to make him wait until you tell him he can go, but still retain his enthusiasm. Many beginners who have been doing well up to this stage come unstuck at this point. Why? Because they are in too big a hurry, put the brake on too quickly and are too hard on their puppy.

Take your puppy on to open ground where he will have no problem in seeing the dummy. Sit your boy down and just loop the lead around his neck, holding the two ends in your left hand. Toss a dummy out ten to fifteen yards, at the same time giving the command 'Sit'. Don't hold him too long, literally only four or five seconds, then drop the lead and give the command. 'Hi lost' with all the umph and enthusiasm you can put into it. Should he hesitate and seem confused, the chances are you've held him too long. In that case run forward with him and, if he doesn't pick up the dummy, do so yourself and throw it for him at once, encouraging him to run in; whatever you do, don't dampen his enthusiasm. Then try again, this time letting him go as, or fractionally before, the dummy hits the ground. If this works well, hold him a couple of seconds longer the next time and then SLOWLY build up the waiting time. When he makes no attempt to move, sit him down and position yourself a few feet in front of him. Throw the dummy, but don't take your eyes off him; if you are out in an open bit of ground it is immaterial how far or where the dummy goes. Your job is to see that he does not run in. If he attempts to go, grab him and put him back on his bottom with a harsh 'No, Sit'. If all is well, send him for the dummy after a few seconds. If, however, he does give you the slip and gets the dummy before you can get to him, don't scold him once he has it. Start again; if again he is too quick for you, then it's a case of back to the lead until it is firmly instilled in his mind that he doesn't go until you say so.

Of course, you may have a smart Alec who is so keen that he'll duck out of the loop made with the lead and be gone. Once he's learned how, that method of restraint is out. You now have two choices. You can put a collar on him, which you can hold whilst you throw a dummy. Alternatively, revert to the check-cord, bringing him up short after he's gone six to eight feet. Then you can unceremoniously put him back where he's supposed to be. Two or three lessons like this should have him sitting until he's told to go. However, if you've got a dog who persistently runs in if he's not on a check-cord, then you've got to get your running shoes on and get after him. As one book that I read on training many years ago said – I can't remember which – you rush out roaring. Stop him getting the dummy, grab him, put the choke-chain on him and yank him back to where he should be, give him a good shake and, in your harshest voice, tell him, 'Sit'. Of course, if he gets to the dummy before you, you're stymied – you have got to beat him to it! Frankly, with a Golden, I would be very surprised if you had to use extreme measures, but you must get him steady before you can advance with your training programme.

When your puppy makes no attempt to run in, then you can further develop the run back. Make him sit off the lead, throw the dummy a few yards and make him walk off with you, at heel. When you have gone a similar distance to that which you have been sending him when letting him off the lead, make him sit and, after a short pause, give the command 'Go back'. When you start doing this, be very watchful that he is at heel as you walk away from the dummy. If you think he's about to take off, quickly tell him, 'Heel'. When he has this firmly established in his memory bank, take the exercise two stages further. Sit him down and walk a few yards away from him. Turn and throw the dummy back over his head, then call him up to heel – but watch it, there is a great temptation to him to run in when you first do this. In doing this you are increasing his steadiness and instilling the fact that he picks up nothing unless you say so. When you reach the point from where you propose sending him back, tell him to sit. Leaving him, walk on a few yards, turn and, with an overhead wave, like throwing a ball, give the command he already knows, 'Go back'. He may well just sit and look at you the first time. It's a new signal and he may not be sure what you mean. If this does happen, move back towards him, continuing to give the signal and verbal instruction, 'Go back.' There may be a little hesitation to start with, but he should quickly get the message. Once he does, keep moving farther and farther away before sending him. In doing this you are developing his memory, enforcing the lesson already taught – to sit and stay – and encouraging him to watch for signals, an all-important point for the future.

You can further extend the run back as he becomes more experienced. Let him see you toss the dummy into some cover where he will not be able to see it and where he will have to hunt and use his nose to find it. You can develop this so that eventually you have your puppy going back 100 to 150 yards. Finally, let him see you put a dummy in a bush or hedge some two feet off the ground and send him back for it. Then go higher until, sometimes he has to stand on his hind legs to reach it. This is a very useful exercise. Once, when mine was the fourth dog to be tried, I put three dogs out of a Field Trial with a bird hung up in a bush. All three had got wind of the bird but, although they hunted the whole area, they could not find it. My dog tried the ground, equally without success, put his head up and then stood on his hind legs; his head disappeared into the bush and he reappeared with a hen pheasant!

Once your puppy is steady, your next task is to teach him to mark, that is, to watch and know exactly where something has fallen, be it a bird or dummy. This is the most important exercise and, obviously, has to be done where there is some cover on the ground; otherwise, it is a seen retrieve. Don't go off into very heavy cover. Ideally, to start, use long grass that he can see over so that he can watch the dummy to within a couple of feet or less of the ground. As far as distance is concerned, twenty to twenty-five yards is quite enough to begin with. At this stage, distance is of no importance; you want him to learn to watch the dummy, know exactly where it fell and be able to go straight to it when you tell him. In this latter connection, to begin with don't hold him too long, so that he loses his concentration on the fall. Equally, don't send him so quickly that it virtually amounts to an instructed run in. To begin with, he could well take the right line but stop short of the fall and start to hunt for the dummy. The reason for this is that his view, being so much nearer the ground than yours is foreshortened. If you don't believe me, get down to his level and have a look for yourself; his view of things is very different from yours! However, he will quickly adjust to this and will soon be going straight to the fall.

The exercise is about marking, so if he misses the dummy completely don't let him gallop around all over the place. Call him back, pick up the dummy and start again. However, should he fail and start to hunt within the area where the dummy fell, leave him alone; indeed, encourage him. Only call him up when it is obvious that he has given up seriously trying and is intent on enjoying himself. What is meant by within the area? As long as he does not get more than about twenty-five yards away and keep returning close to the spot where the dummy fell, let him hunt. This brings us to another point; YOU too have to mark and know where the dummy is so that you can collect it if he cannot find it. Later particularly if you become involved in working tests or field trials, this will become more important. There will be times when you have to direct your dog to the fall when he has been unable to see it. So, learn to mark; you'd be surprised how many beginners launch a dummy into space, haven't a clue where it is and yet expect their puppy to know exactly!

Once your puppy has mastered the art of going straight to the fall, you can begin to increase the distance up to about forty yards. Now, it is quite possible that you will not be able to throw a dummy that far. What do you do? You sit your puppy down and, making sure he remains sitting, walk forward some fifteen or twenty yards. Call 'Mark', so as to be sure he is looking and throw the dummy away from him. The last comment you may think unnecessary, but is it? A lady came to me once for help; she couldn't, apparently, throw the dummy more than twelve to fifteen yards. She assured me her dog was steady. I explained to her about walking forward and throwing the dummy and then moved off to the side. I watched her purposefully walk twenty-five paces, turn and shout 'Mark', and then she threw the dummy straight at her dog! It did prove one thing: he was rock steady! Obviously, you throw the dummy away from him, but slightly at an angle so that you are not inhibiting his view. Return to your puppy as quickly as you can, but without running and getting him all excited, and send him. If everything goes according to plan, continue with this exercise as part of your regular training programme. At this stage each new exercise should become an integral part of his regular workouts, every stage in his education being dependent on the previous one. However, vary the distance and the density and type of cover used. Regarding the former, particularly if you are considering field trialling, make sure he will pick a close mark as well as a long one. You may well say, 'Yes, of course', but if you practise long marks only, there is a real chance that he may ignore something ten yards away.

I had this well demonstrated to me many years ago. I had a really hard-going dog and he would mark quite literally to the inch a couple of hundred yards away. I practised long marks with him a lot (I had a friend throwing the dummy for me) and, I may as well be honest, I liked showing off with him! I was running him in a trial and knew that short of some silly mistake we had the trial in the bag. On the final round, before the run off, I was the only one left to have a retrieve and, consequently, was moved to the centre of the line. We were walking a field of long grass and reeds; there was plenty of game but the shooting left much to be desired. We went on and on, my lad getting more hotted up by the minute, and finally a hen pheasant was hit. I watched it carefully; it made the end of the field some 150 yards away and dropped into the hedge. I was sure it was a dead bird, I knew my dog had marked it and I was expecting to be told to send my dog, but no such luck. The judges obviously thought differently about the bird from the way I did. Within seconds a pheasant got up on the right and flew across the line. It was shot by the flanking gun and dropped some ten yards in front of me. It was almost in a direct line with the bird in the hedge. It was getting late, the judge apologised for the nearness of the retrieve and told me to send my dog. I did. He was level with the near bird, the one he was supposed to pick, within about a fifth of a second. He gave it a cursory glance and was gone before I could get my whistle to my mouth. It was no good blowing, for even if I could have stopped him, which I doubt, and brought him back to pick the bird close to us, he had already blinked it – that is, seen it and left it – and would, therefore, be out of the stake. He was back with the one from the hedge in less time than it has taken me to write this. Ever since then I've trained on long and also very short marks.

Now, amongst your equipment I said you wanted an old tennis-racket and some tennis-balls. The time to bring them into use is once your puppy is marking spot-on. Before you actually hit a ball for your pup, take the racket out on a few training sessions, sit him down and wave it around a bit, to get him used to it. He could well be wary of it to start with, particularly if you've clobbered him for some previous misdemeanour. Before hitting balls into cover, take your pup on to some open ground where he can see them and let him watch them bounce and roll; get him keen on them. When he's retrieved a few from the open, start hitting some into cover for him, but, remember, not more than twenty-five to thirty yards. Don't let your muscles get the better of you! A tennis-ball is going to be a lot harder to find in the rough than a dummy, so a little added scent will not come amiss. He's already used to your scent on the dummies, they acquire that by the mere fact of your handling them. The chances are that you'll be doing this early training in the summer and will, therefore, get a bit hot and sweaty, so stick a couple of balls under your armpits before you use them! I'm not making unkind assumptions about your standards of hygiene; the human scent is very strong. If your lad has any sort of a nose he'll wind them yards away. By 'any sort of nose', I am referring to his ability to smell something. Dogs, like humans, vary in their olfactory ability. 'Wind', of course, means to smell whatever it is that he is retrieving.

From now on, the same rules apply as when you throw a dummy for him. I am repeating myself again, and as before it is intentional; don't be tempted as yet to go for long retrieves. Keep his work fairly close so that if he starts getting out of line you can get after him. Remember, training is basically all about you imposing your will upon your pupil. If you slog a ball seventy to eighty yards away and he over-runs it, it will be only seconds before he's a hundred yards away and what hope have you of imposing your will then? The golden rule is, however well he's going, keep him close. Long marks come into advanced training when your dog is fully on the whistle, which is something I will deal with later.

Now some of you will have heard about dummy launchers and may well have seen one in use; others won't know what they are, and a good thing too! They are an instrument that launches a specially designed dummy into space with the aid of a .22 cartridge and they will, if used to the maximum, put a dummy far beyond the desired distance for your pup, and indeed beyond his ability to retrieve at this stage. Further, they really excite a puppy and before you know it your puppy will be running in! Yes, they have their uses, but not in early or intermediate training. They can be used later for long retrieves in crops such as sugar-beet, and also for putting a dummy across a river or well out into a lake, but at present it is best that you forget about them.

So far all your puppy's retrieves have been seen. Yes, I know he's had to use his nose and hunt to find some of the marks and run backs, but he has known that there was something there; he saw you throw it! Now you have to teach him to hunt without seeing anything and to rely on his nose, not his eyes, to find whatever you have put out to be retrieved. A little forethought over this will make your task that much easier. When you let him have a gallop after a training session, always start it with the command 'Get on' or, if you prefer, 'Get out'. Try to confine this to two or three places and to where there is some cover on the ground. It doesn't take many inches of grass to hide a dummy. To start teaching him to find unseen retrieves, you really require eight or ten dummies

Dual Ch and Ir Dual Ch David of Westley (Sire Ch Dorcas Glorious of Slat, dam Ch Susan of Westley). The only Golden ever to gain this distinction. Owner Miss L. Ross. Breeder Miss J. Gill.

Ir Ch and Ch Bryanstown Gale Warning. (Sire Ir Ch Bryanstown Shannon of Yeo, dam Ir Ch Bryanstown Camrose Gail) BOB GRC Ch Club Show and 4th Irish Retriever Championships 1970. Winner of 11 CCs, 11 Green Stars, 10 Field Trial awards including 1st in A.V. Retriever Stake. Owner/Breeder Mr and Mrs M F. Twist.

if you are going to do the job properly. I can hear you saying, 'But I've only got four, as you recommended.' Don't panic; you want some for temporary use only, and you can easily make some. Get a few old socks and stuffy them very tight with newspaper; that will suffice for what is required. Make sure that when used the dummies carry plenty of scent. You can get bottles of Pheasant Training Scent from Turner Richards, but, quite honestly, although useful, it's not like the real thing nor is it as strong as human scent. I have tried on several occasions, in sugar-beet, putting out two dummies very close to one another, one that I have tucked under my arm as I have walked up the field and one treated with Pheasant Training Scent. Every time the former has been the first dummy picked!

Now, when you come to start on this all-important lesson, stop for a moment and think. First, you want your puppy to go galloping off and hunting, so, to begin with, make this your first exercise so he will be full of 'go' and have plenty of steam in the boiler.

Secondly, you are about to ask your puppy to find a dummy by using his nose only, and when he has no idea that there is anything to be found. How does his nose tell him the dummy is there? 'Simple', you will reply, 'Its scent will be carried to him by the wind.' Exactly, therefore you want the wind blowing from the dummies towards him, so he is what is described as down wind. If he is up wind, the scent is being blown away from him. Make sure then, when you start this exercise, that the wind is blowing from the dummies towards the spot from where you are going to tell him, 'Get on'. This should be the place you normally let him run from, but wait until conditions are right. When they are, get your dummies and lay them out some twenty-five to thirty yards from your sending point, in a half-circle. Be very careful to place the dummies in such away that there is no fear of his running on to another dummy when retrieving the one he has found and bringing it to you. If he does do this it is almost a certainty that he will change dummies, that is, drop the one he's carrying and pick another. That is a cardinal sin. To change birds in a field trial or dummies in a working test is an eliminating offence, so just make sure it cannot occur! If it should happen, you cannot do a lot about it at this stage, for you have sent him out to find something; in his book he's done even better and found two things! If you read the Riot Act now, he'll associate it with going out and hunting, so just let it go for the present. Normally, it is not too difficult a fault to rectify.

By the way, if you go by car to your training ground, make sure you don't park it where your lad can sit and watch your preparations for his unseen retrieve. It can happen; I've seen it done. If one of your play areas is just where you come through a gate or gap in a hedge, so much the better, because normally that will mean he will be running off into an area 180° in front of you and will not be able to get behind you. If you've put the dummies out correctly, he's bound to find one. As soon as he does, whistle him back and make a great fuss of him, then send him off again at once. There is a chance that he'll hesitate, because something is different. Should this happen, just stand there quietly for minute or two and ignore him. Then, suddenly, tell him, 'Get on'. If you've timed it right, he'll have had enough of standing around and will be gone. Let him have two or three retrieves and then call it a day. The only difference between the first and subsequent retrieves is that you should change your command to 'Hi lost get on'. He should already be associating 'Hi lost' with the fact that there is something to be found, because that is what you've been saying to him prior to sending him off for marks. Once he has got the idea of going out without seeing anything thrown, you can dispense with the 'Get on'. When he's picked whatever you decide to let him have, put him in the car, or take him back to the house or kennel, and collect the remaining dummies. Return to the same place the following day and go through the same procedure. If he's really keen, he'll remember, and as soon as you tell him to go he'll be gone like the proverbial bullet. If possible, the next time go to a different place. You don't want him to start associating being sent for unseen retrieves with just one place.

Once he's going out without any bother, and this should be in only a matter of days, you can dispense with the temporary dummies and just put out two or three. Further, make him sit before you send him. Finally, cut down to one dummy. However, be careful he doesn't go galloping off out of the area. If he does, whistle him back immediately. You should know, by now, that if he does not respond you must go out after him.

So far, so good. However, up to now his unseen retrieves are ones you could have picked up yourself. It is now time to take him into woodland or some heavier cover, not too thick but enough to make him really hunt. When you start this, again no great distances will be involved but, so you do not lose your dummies, it is a good idea to tie strips of white cloth or bandage to branches close to or over the dummies. Once you start working in real cover, revert to using all four dummies. You don't want him coming back without anything if you can possibly avoid it. In this connection, make sure the dummies are carrying plenty of scent. Incidentally, don't put the markers so low that he can easily see them. If you do, he'll start to remember that white markers mean a dummy and then he'll go straight to them and not bother to hunt.

As he becomes more and more proficient, you should put the dummies further and further into the wood, providing you are sat-isfied that he is genuinely hunting and not just galloping around. This is one situation in which I let a youngster go well away from me. He has got to learn to hunt on his own and out of sight of you. Put three or four dummies out still, parallel with the point from which you are sending him, so that there is no risk of his running on to a second dummy once he's found one. Don't overdo it. If he's pulled off a good retrieve, call it a day and pick up the others. To save time, I number the dummies with a felt pen so I know which one has been picked and don't have to waste time looking.

Up to this point, it has been assumed that you have let your puppy gallop around from the earliest possible moment and, therefore, will have no problem in getting him out. However, I am absolutely certain there will be those who, for various reasons – chiefly through being too hard or in too much of a hurry – will by now have their dog glued to their side and won't get out unless he sees something thrown. This, as I intimated earlier, is not an easy problem to overcome and will almost certainly take quite a time to correct. It has to be assumed that the puppy in question has plenty of get up and go and is just confused as to when he is supposed to use it. If he is a walker, even to a seen retrieve, I doubt whether it is worth struggling on; obviously he has no great interest in his job and has just pottered out to please when something has been thrown. However, if he has plenty of drive but does not know when he can use it, then there are several course open.

First, if he is a kennel dog, then your job is made that much easier, although the same criteria can be applied, to a lesser degree, to a house dog. Simply don't take him out for a week or ten days. Get him absolutely bursting for exercise! Put some dummies out as already described, release him and tell him 'Get on'. With any luck at all, he'll rush off and on to a dummy. Let him pick as many as he likes. The moment he stops, put him on the lead and take him home. Another few days confined to barracks and then out you go again, of course, to the same place. This is a case for constant repetition until he knows that when you say 'Get on', it means he's got to get out and hunt. This is something which, I am glad to say, I haven't had much experience of, but the above worked very well with a friend's Labrador. Secondly, if it is impossible for you to get your lad so that he is bursting for exercise, or it may be your nature is such that you would not like to confine him to barracks, you could try the following. Many years ago, in the days when I had only trained two or three dogs, I had a super Golden bitch. I was in too big a hurry and, by the time she was a year old, I could not get her to hunt unless a gun was fired or she had seen something fall. There was no book available to tell me what to do, so I had to figure something out for myself. I made up a lot of dummies, spread them around in the corner of a field and literally walked her on to one. She picked it, I ran off and she followed. Then we did it all again and again and again. We did it for about ten days. Then I took her to the place where I'd been doing this, and a soon as I said 'Hi lost', she was gone. From then on she never looked back; she won ten or twelve field trial awards and was a super wild-fowling dog.

If you are in the fortunate position of having a friend with a trained dog then, once again, you could ask for help. Your puppy will almost certainly range out when the older dog does and, once it is established that he can do this, he'll start going out on his own. Finally, you can try a bit of bluff. Sit your pup down and walk forward and drop a dummy so that he can see it. Don't throw it like a normal mark, just hold it out at arm's length and drop it. Go back and send him. Do this a number of times, always in the same place, but not all on the one day, spread it over perhaps a week. Then walk forward and, turning your back to your puppy, drop the dummy so he doesn't see it. Return to him and tell him, 'Get on'. Training being largely a matter of repetition, it will have become fixed in his memory that when you go to that particular spot there will be a dummy to retrieve. Your troubles should then be largely over, for if you repeat the latter part of this ruse over several more days, he will associate the place with a retrieve. Then, finally, put out a few dummies, give the command 'Hi lost get on' and, if you have any luck at all, he'll be out and back with a dummy in no time. From then on it is back to normal training for unseen retrieves.

To have reached this stage will have taken a good three to four months. Consolidate this work before moving on.

8

Advanced Training

By now you should have an obedient but, I trust, exuberant dog, who is rapidly beginning to believe that the sun rises and sets in you. Keep it that way!

Your next task is to introduce him to gunfire; this is where your .22 starting pistol comes in. The vast majority of retrievers are not gun-shy, but quite a few to begin with are gun-nervous. There is a big difference between the two! The latter show uncertainty, indeed surprise, which is not unreasonable when the pleasant tranquillity of a summer's evening is suddenly shattered by a loud bang. Such dogs may appear startled but, if off the lead, they will not run away. The truly gun-shy dog tucks his tail between his legs and runs, sometimes towards home but frequently simply in a wild panic. It is my belief that the majority of gun-shy dogs are made that way through stupidity, rather than through an inherited failing, though the latter can be the cause. Some people introduce a puppy to gunfire at a very early age. I find that around 10 or 11 months is quite soon enough, unless you have any doubts. Doubts could be because of apparent excessive nervousness on the part of your pup if you drop a feeding tin, or someone bangs a door, or even if the popping of a champagne cork is heard! If you suspect that he might be gun-shy you should test your puppy as soon as possible; there is no point in putting in hours of work to make a gundog of him if the one thing he cannot stand is a gun!

To test him you will need help; someone to fire the pistol for you. Take him out to your training area and, if you've gone by car, leave the door open so that he can get in should he take fright. It is far better that he should do this than go tearing off across the countryside, which could result in an accident. Walk him away from the car and, when you have gone about fifty yards, sit him down. Your assistant should go on a further hundred yards or so and, on a given signal from you, fire the pistol. If the puppy remains sitting, no problem. Should he jump up to you, seeking reassurance, he may be a bit gun-nervous and, consequently, you will have to take care training him to the gun, but there is nothing to worry about. However, should he set off for the car at a rate of knots and neither heed your whistle nor your calls, then you certainly have a problem – and a big one! Frankly, I do not think it is worth trying to develop his future as a working gundog. There are few more miserable spectacles than a truly gun-shy dog being dragged around at a shoot on a lead! My advice would be to find him a nice suburban home and start again.

However, you may be so attached to your pooch by this time that you will wish to have a try at overcoming his phobia. You might just be lucky if you have endless patience and are prepared to work at it. The first thing to do is to find someone with a trained dog. Arm yourself with a child's cap-pistol, that will give plenty of bang at this stage, and let the two dogs have a gallop. When they are a good distance from you, fire the pistol. The older dog will almost certainly come galloping back. Hopefully, at the worst, the puppy will stay where he is; at the best he will follow. If he follows, bang off one more cap; that will be quite enough for now. Don't get carried away and start blazing away as though you were taking part in Custer's last stand! If you are fortunate and he comes back to you, give him much praise, and go through the same routine the next day and for many more to come. Increase the number of caps you fire as he becomes less concerned and eventually revert to the .22. A word of caution: when you do this, make sure that your puppy is well away from you when you fire the first cartridge. If you get a favourable reaction, then it's a case of going over the course again, using the louder bang, until he is only a matter of yards from you. If you achieve this, you have won. I knew a springer bitch whose owner cured her of being gun-shy by this method – it took him seven months!

The only other suggestion I can make is to have someone banging away at feeding time. This is the same principle. Fire one or two caps, well away, as you give your puppy his food. Continue over the weeks, making more bangs and getting nearer. Build up an association of bangs with food. After a while, a few bangs to indicate that it is feeding time can help. However, if after this you try your puppy with another dog and he takes off again, or is so terrified that he won't eat his food, then honestly I don't think it worth the worry either to you or him to continue.

Assuming you have no suspicions about your lad's reaction to a gun, make a start on this stage when he's 10 or 11 months old. Follow the procedure I have already described; if he does not worry, then it is a comparatively quick exercise. As I have said, to start with some help will be useful and certainly an 11- or 12-year-old child could do all that is required. But a word of warning; even a

Ch Rayleas Reema (Sire Sebastian of Eidrah, dam Rayleas Spring Song). Leading Dual-Purpose Golden 1985 and 1986 Owner/Breeder Mrs C. Hardie.

blank cartridge gives quite a forceful explosion. After all, only about three times the amount of powder in a blank is required to drive the captive bolt of a humane-killer through the skull of a bullock or horse! Therefore, avoid any possible situation in which two children could be squabbling over who fires the pistol. Should one get a hand over the hole in the top of the barrel, through which the force of the blast passes, and the other child pulls the trigger, what happens could be nasty. I once saw something of this nature happen; the result was distressing to say the least. Anyway, you don't want any arguments going on; they will distract your pupil.

According to the reaction you get to the first shot, plan your gun training programme. If it is one of interest and, possibly, surprise, but not fear, then you can rapidly bring your gunman, the person with the gun, nearer until, after a week or ten days, the pistol is being fired only a few yards away. If there is a slightly nervous reaction, then follow the same procedure, but take things more slowly. Plenty of assurance and encouragement is required; even the occasional tidbit is permitted. When your gunman has moved in to about thirty yards away, get him/her to fire the pistol and throw a dummy, quickly moving back out of the way. Send your puppy; if he goes without any hesitation and makes a nice retrieve, you've no further worries and you can do the rest on your own. From now on, when training generally, sit your puppy and move forward. Instead of shouting 'Mark', fire your pistol and throw a dummy. Then go back and send him in the normal way. Don't do this every training session. You don't want him starting to think that there must be a 'bang' before there is something to retrieve. In dog training parlance, too much banging at an early age will hot him up and he'll start running in. Take your time, as in everything else in training, until you can fire the pistol a few yards from him without getting a reaction. From now on, much depends on your circumstances but, whatever they are, when you introduce him to a 12-bore shotgun, just keep your distance to start with.

Whilst you have been introducing your puppy to gunfire, you should have been practising and developing the exercises he has learned to date. By now he should be so much your dog that having other people around is no distraction. This is as it should be and, henceforth, some occasional help can be most useful. Indeed, if you have a friend who is also training a gundog, you can get together from time to time. If you do this, don't let any element of competition creep in. What you do together should be purely to hold a training session, not to conduct a private working test where you start trying to go one better than each other. If you do that, sooner or later, you'll certainly ask something of your puppy which he hasn't the experience to respond to. Do this and you could retard your training programme. Any get-togethers for a workout in company should not, at this stage, be on a regular basis. The main part of your training still needs to be done in private, so that you can command his full attention.

As I said at the end of the last chapter, you have now reached a stage where you should consolidate what has been learned, until it has become second nature. At the same time you can develop some of the exercises. Take marks, for example. So far your puppy has been sitting before the dummy has been thrown. Now start walking up rough pieces of ground and, suddenly, whilst you are still walking, call 'Mark' and throw a dummy out in front. This is both a test of his steadiness not to run in and a development of his alertness. Up to now there has been a build-up to retrieves and he has grown to know what's coming. Now, without any preamble, you spring one on him. You have to teach him, and he has to learn, to be watchful all the time. This is an exercise in which, after the initial retrieves, a helper can be most useful. Have him walking along some thirty yards ahead of you and to the side. Get him without warning to call 'Mark' and throw a dummy. Two or three times each session will be enough. If you have assistance you can now gradually increase the distance of the marks, up to seventy to eighty yards. Don't forget the odd very close one!

When this is going well, take your pup out on his own and introduce another new element. As you are walking along, let your lad see you drop a dummy. Don't throw it, just drop it by your side. Walk on about fifteen yards, throw another dummy forward, and turn and send your puppy for the one you dropped, with the command 'Hi lost go back'. He may have a strong inclination to circle round and head for the second dummy – the one you threw forward. Stop any such move with a sharp 'No' and be on your blocks ready for a quick sprint to stop him if necessary. Of course, you've a 50 per cent chance that he'll happily go for the first one, but whatever happens, that is the one he MUST pick up, even if you walk him virtually back on top of it. When he's picked it, if you've moved, return to where you were and send him for the mark. The chances are that he'll have forgotten exactly where it is, but let him hunt as long as he stays in the area. Advance this exercise by increasing the distance he has to go back, still letting him see you drop the dummy and, also, increasing the distance of the mark. He will quickly catch on and go racing back for it. Similarly, he will remember where the dummy is in front. The next step is to drop a dummy without his seeing it. Go on a short distance and send him back. If you've done your job properly this should cause him no trouble. It is, after all, only an unseen retrieve and he's become used to going back anyway. Having done a few of these blinds, repeat the exercise, but with a mark forward as well. Normally there is no problem over this, for he will remember that when you send him back there is something there and he knows there is a dummy in front.

Up to now, marking has been straightforward, with no obstacles. The time has come to introduce a few hazards. As the first one, I suggest a good thick hedge. Sit your puppy down some twenty to twenty-five yards away from it and lob a dummy over to the far side. Don't delay many seconds before sending him. He has to find a way through the hedge and possibly to negotiate a ditch as well. When he reaches the hedge, give the command 'Get over'. Use this on all occasions when you want your dog to cross something, be it a hedge, wire fence, gate or river. If he jibs at the idea of pushing through an unaccustomed barrier, go forward, encouraging him. Find a place where the cover is less thick and, if he is still being difficult, throw another dummy over so that he not only sees it but hears it land as well. If you have to do this, don't check him, let him run in if he will! Should things get really sticky, collect a few stones and throw them through the hedge – anything as long as you get him to the other side! However, as he should have been retrieving dummies from reasonably heavy cover by now you shouldn't have too much trouble getting him through. A word of warning: don't choose a hedge which you frequently go through via a gate or gap. Even if this is a hundred yards or more away, the chances are that your boy will take the easy road if he doesn't care a lot for the obstacle that you have asked him to tackle. He may not be able to reason but he's got a good memory! Therefore, if at all possible choose a hedge that he does not know.

It will not be long before he's pushing through hedges without any fuss. The next step is to find a wire fence along the edge of a wood or enclosing a young plantation. Take your puppy close to this and sling a dummy over. If he's well on with his jumping, there should be no problem. Should he fail to jump it, heave him over and, when he has picked the dummy, start to walk away. If he lacks confidence he'll probably put his paws up on the top, run up and down and generally be rather stupid. However, keep walking and keep calling; sooner or later he's going virtually to tumble over the fence and join you. If you run into a problem, it's just a question of patience and repetition until he gets it right.

In the previous chapter I mentioned the sin of changing retrieves. Training has advanced sufficiently for attention to now be given to this – a most important point. Take your puppy out on to open ground, where he can easily see the dummies. Sit him down, move about fifteen yards away and throw a dummy out either side of him – not too close, at least ten yards away at this stage – and whistle him to you. If he as much as looks at either of the dummies as he is coming in, immediately berate him with a stern 'No'. If he looks as though he is going to lift one of the dummies, rush out and stop him. If he beats you to it, well, the rules haven't changed. Thank him for the dummy and start again, but stay a bit closer this time. As soon as he realises that he is not to touch the dummies, throw them nearer to him and move further away yourself.

When you have achieved this, leave him sitting, walk away from him, tossing out dummies right and left so that you make a lane eight or ten yards wide, then call him to you. If he looks as though he is going to deviate from a straight run, a quick 'No' should stop him. To take the exercise to its finale, give him a longish mark, then when he is coming back throw a dummy in his general direction but, to start with, well out of his path. As you practise this you can get nearer and nearer to his return route, but don't precipitate trouble by landing one right in front of him. Later you should be able to do that if you wish, for by then it will be so embedded in his memory that he does not touch anything if he is already retrieving that he will treat such a diversion with positive contempt.

Another temptation you can put in his path, literally, is to get someone to bowl a reasonably large ball across in front of him as he is returning with a retrieve. If the bowler is out of sight, so much the better; that gives a greater element of surprise. This diversion is far more likely to make your boy fall from grace than throwing dummies around. If he does fall, then get after him at once with much vocal admonishment, grab him, give him a good shake and take him back, without ceremony, to where he dropped the dummy. After a few minutes have a repeat performance, but this time be ready to shout 'No' the moment the ball appears, heading across his path. He may have another go, but that is unlikely if you made your displeasure forceful enough. However, if he does, get after him again and again until such time as he appreciates that he does not chase things when he is retrieving. Some people, myself amongst them, have tried a dummy on a length of strong elastic. This is stretched across the return path of your dog and, as he is coming back you release it by a pull on a cord. The dummy, usually clad in a rabbit skin, comes whizzing across in front of your puppy, who may be tempted to sin once, but if you administer the right deterrent that will not happen again. To start with, the lure is going very fast, and, secondly puppies quickly associate the lure with trouble. However, if it has given you the opportunity to fix firmly in his memory that he doesn't chase when retrieving it has served its purpose.

The time has come to introduce your puppy to feather. You require two wings, preferably pheasant, but that doesn't really matter. I do not, as I have already said, like white ones. They are all right for the initial introduction, but if you are working with feathered dummies they do show up and puppies are inclined to go looking for them rather than hunting for them – a big difference! Attach the wings to a dummy with a couple of strong elastic bands; make sure that these are really tight. If not, when you throw the dummy and it hits the ground, the wings will fly off. That is a horrible pun, but it is also a reality and it will give a choice of retrieves for your lad should you be silly enough to send him. I have seen both the wings come off, and land several feet from the dummy, so make sure it doesn't happen to you. Before throwing the winged dummy, offer it to your pup. Let him sniff it and, if he wants to, take it in his mouth and let him hold it. Once he's become accustomed to the different taste and fell in his mouth, there shouldn't be any problem. Occasionally one comes upon a puppy who doesn't want to know. If this happens, gently put your prepared dummy in his mouth, make him hold it, and walk backwards away from him with your hand under his jaw as you make him carry it. I can only ever remember once having real trouble over this and then the puppy gave me the solution. He had been spitting out the winged dummy as often as he could over the previous week. We were out for a walk, and all the dogs were having a good gallop, when suddenly he came racing back to me with a very dead blackbird! He was extremely pleased with himself and I gratefully received his offering and put it in the pocket of any old jacket – high though it was! When we got home I took the wings off the long-deceased bird and, with difficulty, affixed them to a dummy. I threw it for my puppy, who retrieved it without hesitation. I added the pheasant wings, keeping the blackbird's on to of them – still no problem. I then removed the latter, rubbed the remainder of the blackbird over the pheasant wings and tried again.

Mrs Val Birkin's Ch Sansue Golden Ruler, one of the 'greats' of the 1980s and 1990s. Apart from winning 31 CCs, including BOB at Crufts, even more importantly, he sired numerous CC winners, several at Crufts, including the 1994 BOB winner.

The result was a quick and immediate retrieve and the puppy never looked back.

There may be those amongst you who have been wondering what the point of all this is. It is to prepare your puppy for the time he is asked to retrieve cold game and subsequently hot birds. We know that there is a great difference in the feel of canvas and of feathers and we detect that with our hands. Imagine the difference we would notice if, like our dogs, we were asked to take them in our mouths!

9

Working for A-Levels

If your puppy is coming up to expectation in respect of what you have been teaching him, his responses being immediate and his retrieves quick and well-delivered, then you can claim he's passed his O-levels and the time has come to consider his further education. By the way, it may have occurred to some readers that I am still referring to your dog as a puppy. The reason is that, in the eyes of the Kennel Club, he is classified as a puppy in relation to Field Trialling. Their definition reads, 'A puppy is a dog whelped not earlier than 1 January in the year preceding the date of the Field Trial, but in any stake run in January a dog which was a puppy in the previous month shall be deemed a puppy.' It is quite easy to follow when you read it slowly. For example, a puppy born in, say March, 1987 remains a puppy to the end of 1988. However, should you run him in a Field Trial in January 1989, for this purpose he would be deemed to be a puppy still. It might help to add that the Field Trial season for retrievers finishes at the end of January. So, although your lad could be well over 12 months old, from a work point of view he is still a puppy.

Your training programme from now on depends largely upon what your ultimate objective is and on the standard of excellence you require. Should your aim be to have an obedient shooting companion, then there is no great point in starting higher education and trying for what I will call A-levels. The average shooting man's dog does not get asked to carry out the sort of retrieves that require such training. I have said 'average' because there are some shooting men who demand the highest Field Trial standards and thoroughly understand good dog work, but, alas, their number is limited. Over the past fifty years or more, I have seen a very large number of good gundogs. The vast majority were excellent game-finders but would have been totally at sea running in a field trial as, indeed, would their owners – that is a completely different ball game. For example, on a shoot, if birds have been dropping into a wood behind the line of guns, when the drive is over the party will almost certainly walk to edge of the wood before their dogs are sent. The dogs will normally never be more than about thirty-five or forty yards from their owners, except when working on a runner. They will get launched into the wood and clear it with the minimum of help and attention from their bosses, many of whom will be chatting and laughing with fellow guests. In a trial, under similar circumstances, you would probably be asked to send your dog from where the guns had been standing and for a specific bird – a cock pheasant that fell by a certain tree, say, or a hen that landed on the edge of the wood and was seen to run. Again, on a normal day's shooting where birds had dropped out on an open field, the guns would walk out across this, their dogs ranging in front of them, picking game as they went. In a trial you could be asked to send your dog over distances of 150 yards or more for a specified bird and to handle, that is direct, your dog to it. As I have said, these are two different approaches to the same job.

Before moving on, this is as good a place as any to mention Training Classes, of which there are many held up and down the country. Frankly, I have mixed feelings about them. They do a lot of good; equally, they can do a lot of harm. Let me explain. In most cases they are run, or appear to be run, on the assumption that those taking part know something about what they are undertaking, albeit only theory derived from reading a book or two, and they have done some preliminary groundwork with their dog. Frequently this assumption is not justified and, as a result, both owners and dogs are precipitated into attempting exercises for which they are not properly prepared. Ideally, before starting field work, there should be a series of talks, giving a chance for the true novices to ask questions and get some idea about what they are becoming involved in. I know that in some classes this does occur, but it is the exception rather than the rule. I have stressed the importance, particularly in the early days, of training without distractions for your pupil. This is difficult to achieve when a dozen or so other dogs are being trained at the same time with dummy launchers being fired, whistles blown and people shouting commands, and there is the general excitement, for a young dog, of being in the vicinity of a lot of others. I know that there will be those who disagree with me. Fair enough, that's their prerogative, but how many top trainers of field trial dogs can they find who train their puppies in an atmosphere that engenders both with excitement and lack of concentration? As I see it, training classes come into their own when your puppy has the basic rudiments fully stored in his memory and you want to start working him in company.

To continue with the training programme, if you wish to run your boy in Trials or, indeed, Working Tests, then both you and he have

Dual Ch Stubblesdown Golden Lass (Sire Stubbings Golden Garry, dam Stubbings Golden Olympia). One of only two dual champion bitches in the breed in GB. Owner Mr W. E. Hickmott. Breeder F. D. Jessamy.

Ch Deremar Rosemary (Sire Ch Camrose Cabus Christopher, dam Deremar Tess of Farmcott). BOB Crufts 1973. 1st NGR All Aged Stake, 24 dog stake, 19 Field Trial awards. Owner Mrs D. J. Price-Harding. Breeder Mr D. J. Price-Harding.

more to learn. If, on the other hand, your aim is to have a useful shooting dog, you can rest on your laurels until we move on to work with cold game. For those who want to go the full course, the next four lessons are most important ones, hand signals, stopping on the whistle, straight running and taking a line. Those with a limited knowledge (and I don't expect the knowledgeable to be reading this) may have wondered why I have not advocated teaching your puppy to take hand signals before now. The answer is relatively simple. I have not wanted to encourage you to start over-checking your puppy in his formative months as that would lessen his natural drive and enthusiasm. If you had used hand signals too soon you would have stood a very good chance of getting him into the habit of looking to you for help. He must learn to hunt and find things on his own before you start to harness and direct his talent.

To a small degree, you have already been giving your puppy lessons in understanding hand signals. Slapping your thigh to keep

Hand Signals Should Be Clear And Decisive

Sitting – always alert, ready to mark.

Going out at speed on instruction.

Stopping on the whistle – awaiting a signal.

Change of direction – go right.

Returning – a direct line is important.

Delivery – speed should be maintained right to the handler.

him to heel; raising your hand, in the early stages, when making him sit and stay; the overarm action when sending him for a run back and the forward movement of the arm when sending him out for a retrieve are all a start to this. Now you have to teach him to go left, right, back and come in towards you. All signals should be clear and decisive. If you are sending to the right, then snap the arm out to its full extent, even move your foot out and lean the body in the direction you want your puppy to go; as you do this give the command, the same one, 'Hi lost'. Leave your puppy in no doubt that he's got to get out to the right and quickly! Put plenty of zip into both the action and the command. When the lesson has been learned there will be no need to be so forceful. Quieten the command and moderate the movement; he will eventually take the arm signal as sufficient indication of your requirements. So go for it when training, but for goodness sake don't act like a defector from the Russian ballet if you enter a Field Trial or a Working Test! Then, the quieter your handling the better.

Circumstances must determine how you start to teach hand signals. If you are fortunate enough to own a paddock, or have the use of one where you can do as you like, mow some training paths, as shown in the diagram. The main path, A–B, should be about 40 yds long and 6 to 8 ft wide. The path leading to D should be 4 to 6 ft wide and all three, C, D, and E, should be 30 to 35 yds long. The paths to C and E need only be the width of one cut of the mower which, I am assuming will be a rotary one. If you think you can accurately throw a dummy from Z to land on strip D, fine, then by all means keep this path narrow, but you must be sure that the dummy finishes up on the mown area.

When all is ready, take your puppy and sit him at X, so that he faces you. Move to Z and, just to get him acclimatised to your new set-up, lob a dummy over him towards D. There's nothing new about this; it is virtually just a run back. When he's had a couple of these to warm up, still with him at X and you at Z, throw a dummy towards A. Make sure it lands where he can easily see it. Send him for it with the command 'Hi lost' and the exaggerated arm signal to the left, your left. He may be slightly uncertain about what you mean, for, other than for run backs, he has been by your side before when you have sent him for a retrieve or to hunt. If he does stick, move in to him and send him in the way that he is used to. Repeat the exercise but, this time, stand much nearer to him, use the exaggerated arm signal and send him almost as soon as the dummy hits the ground. After two or three such

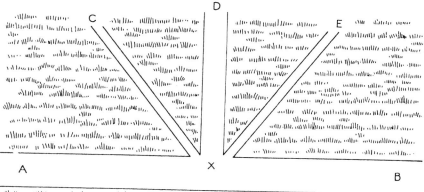

retrieves he should quickly get the idea. Dogs, when first asked to do this exercise, sometimes show a tendency to run to you at Z before heading towards A. Should this happen, stop him and take him back to X. Do not send your pup from Z. You are teaching him to go for a retrieve from a point that you determine, in this case X, and this is where he must go from.

Once he is going from X to the dummy at A and back to you at Z, start working him right to B. When he is retrieving from both points without any problems, throw a dummy to A and B in that order. Move closer to him than you would be at Z, so that you can take immediate action if necessary. When ready, signal him to retrieve the dummy from A – the first one thrown. There will be a strong temptation for him to try for B – the second one. If he attempts this, give a sharp 'No' and quickly stop him. Should you have to do this, once you are again in control send him in the normal way for A. Take him back and sit him at X and return to where you were and send him for B. You'll have no trouble over this, it's the one he's had his mind on since you threw them! When he has picked up both dummies, go through it all again. If he is not retrieving as instructed after three or four goes, call it a day; you don't want to bore him. So that you finish on a good note, give him a mark from the long grass. Continue on the next day, and for as many days as may be necessary, until he is responding automatically to your signals. Usually this exercise is quickly learned but, occasionally, you will get a puppy that has difficulty in grasping what is required. When the message has been got across, alternate the retrieves so that sometimes you send for the first dummy thrown,

87

sometimes the second. Work on this until there is no hesitation and you are satisfied.

To continue the sequence, as before sit your puppy at X and from Z throw a dummy to A or B, it doesn't matter which, and a second towards D. Send him for the latter, using the correct over-head signal and the command, 'Go back'. There could be a slight hesitation, for you have changed the routine to which he has become accustomed when working on the grid. However, push him back and, when he has retrieved this, let him fetch the first one. Do this a few times and then reverse the procedure; that is, get him to retrieve the one at A or B first and then the one at D. When you can ring the changes without problems, put three dummies out – A, B and D. From now on, vary the order in which these are retrieved. To achieve this exercise fully without a hiccup could take several weeks, or it could be a matter of days; it depends entirely on how bright your pup is and on his keenness. Finally, should your dog over-run a retrieve, you want to be able to draw him back towards you. Sit him down at the end of the strip A–B, walk to the farther end and throw a dummy towards him. Then 'pip' him in towards you, at the same time signalling him to do so; that is, stretch your arm out in front of you, a bit below shoulder height and, with fingers spread, bring your hand down towards the ground. As he comes up to the dummy encourage him to pick it up. Once he's had a few retrieves in the open, start doing the same exercise again, but in longish grass where he cannot see the dummy. This too is a natural progression from the exercises you've been doing on the grid. Start throwing the dummies so they land beyond the mown strips A–B and X–D, thus making your puppy do some hunting as well as taking hand signals.

What if you haven't a paddock where you can put paths? Fortunately modern farming has, quite unwittingly, supplied an excellent alternative in corn crops, namely the 'tramlines' used by tractors when spraying the crop.

Now we move on to what, at times, can be a rather delicate exercise for beginners, namely putting your puppy on the whistle. This is training to stop him when out hunting so that you can direct him to the fall of a dummy or bird by the means of hand signals. He already knows that one short blast means he is to sit; stopping on the whistle is purely a progression from this exercise. Why, therefore should I claim that this is a somewhat delicate lesson at times? The answer is that if it is done with too much intensity, you will finish up with your puppy stopping but, because of the way you have gone about it, being confused and on stopping becoming virtually rooted to the spot. One minute you've told him to get out and hunt; the next he gets instructions to sit. So he takes what appears to be the safest course – gets his backside down and keeps it there! I once sent a bitch to a top professional trainer for whom I had, and still have, the very highest regard to get her put on the whistle. My reason for doing this was that I just hadn't time and had reached the stage in her training at which this was the next move. Whatever happened I don't know, but when I said I wanted her back I think nothing much had been done and so she had been given a crash course. She stopped all right, but in no way could I get her going and I never have been able to! If your lad's a toughie, you've no problems, but if, like my bitch and many other Goldens, he's a softie, then have a care!

I normally start stopping a puppy as he is coming towards me. I sit him down and move off ten or twelve paces and whistle him up. Halfway I blow a short sharp blast, which he has got to know means 'sit'. As he is in such close proximity then, that will almost always work. If all goes well, go forward and make a big fuss of him; let him know what a great chap he is. Then move back to where you were and whistle him to you. Repeat this, over a number of days, until he is sitting at the first 'pip' and you have extended the distance. If I've a really keen young dog I will sometimes stop him twice on the run in to me, but it entirely depends on your puppy. The great thing is not to overdo it.

When you have perfected this, it is time to move on to the next part of the exercise – stopping him going away from you. Reflect on what I said in an earlier chapter – anyone can stop a dog, but it's a heck of a job to make one go! So don't, in enforcing your will, stifle his natural enthusiasm and drive. Take him on to a bare bit of ground where he can easily see a dummy, sit him down and throw one. Send him and, as soon as he's gone a few yards, whilst he's still close enough for you to dominate him, blow the stop signal. If you've done the first part properly he will stop immediately. If everything goes as planned, don't hold him long; after a few seconds send him for the dummy. If he hesitates, repeat your command both verbally and by signal. Should this not work, go to him, make a fuss of him and then send him. Keep quietly having a go until you've got it right. When this happens, as in so many other exercises, start increasing the distance. Whatever you do, don't overdo it; if you do you'll have your puppy stopping automatically every time you send him out.

Putting him on the whistle must be a gradual happening; it is not something you can drive home like teaching him to sit or walk at heel. It may be that your puppy is not as biddable as I have intimated he should be and he decides he's not going to stop just because you blow your whistle and say 'Sit'. Should this happen, use your check-cord. If he will not obey when coming to you, have the cord around a post or a tree so you can bring him up short. If he ignores you when going away, stopping him suddenly once or twice should make him realise that you mean business. If you've a really hard-going dog, I suggest you attach the end of the cord to a post or round a tree. Measure how far it will reach, put a marker on the ground and just before he reaches this point when you've sent him for the dummy, give a 'pip' on your whistle. If you've timed it right, he'll remember being brought up short just as you blew that whistle and he'll begin to think it's pretty strong medicine! If you've the type of dog that needs this sort of treatment, make sure he's 'motoring' before being rudely brought to a halt. This is one reason for attaching the end of the cord to a post rather than having it wound round your hand; some seventy pounds of Golden Retriever doing about 28 to 30 mph can give quite a jolt when he reaches the limit! However, it is most unlikely that you will have to resort to such methods.

When he is stopping the moment you 'pip' him up, move on to combining this exercise with hand signals. Send your lad out, stop him with the whistle and throw a dummy away to the side. Then direct him on to it with hand signals, making sure that the dummy is in cover so he has to hunt. This is most important, because once he fully cottons on to the combination of the whistle and hand signals, he could become too reliant on you to find whatever he is sent for. Further, when going out he'll keep stopping and looking back at you for directions, which is what the Americans call 'popping'. It is a very bad fault; it's his job to do the finding!

Really, from now on it is a question of practice, a little but not too often. Remember he now knows what the stop signal is, and he also knows about hand signals. If he ignores either get out after him at once for he is showing his contempt for your authority! As Charles Morgan says in his most excellent book, 'Just one blast, and that's all – then you're on the run, out to get him. To give more encourages disobedience.' Having said this, PLEASE use your whistle as little as possible. Your dog should be the game-finder, not you! There will be many occasions, when working, when he will not be able to see you and get help from you.

Next we come to something dear to my heart, achieving a straight-running dog. What do I mean by this? The answer is exactly what you would think, a dog that goes from 'a' to 'b' in a straight line which, when you 'pip' him up will start to hunt and hold his ground, that is, stay in the same area. That is easy enough on a mark, but not so easy on a blind. Over the years, when judging at Field Trials, I have very often had a handler come into the line with his/her dog and have been able to give accurate information as to where a bird has fallen, then stood back and watched as the dog has gone everywhere except to the fall!

How do you make your dog run straight? I'll tell you. Let's go back to the grid. Sit your puppy at X, walk towards D and, making sure you've got his attention, shout 'Mark' and drop a dummy. Continue back towards him and, when you are about fifteen yards away, drop another. Return to him and line him up, that is, see that he is sitting facing exactly in a straight line with where he has to go. Bend down and make a signal by moving your hand forward by his face, so that your hand and his nose are dead on line for the nearest dummy, then send him. When he has retrieved it, line him up again and send him for the second one. Having done a few runs on X–D, change to either X–C or X–E. At this stage of his training make sure, each time you send him, that he is lined up correctly and make your signal positive. The message that you have to get across is that where your hand is pointing is where he has to go. I'd better, but I shouldn't have to, remind you that this doesn't all have to happen on one day; like all training it takes time and, of course, that all-important ingredient, patience. Three or four runs a session is quite enough.

When he is picking up two dummies well, let him see you drop three dummies. Position the third one (that will be the first one you'll drop) right at the end of the strip you are using. In all probability he will pick up the first two with no problems and start to deviate when going for the third; he could have forgotten it. If this happens, 'pip' him up and bring him back to the path, sit him down about ten yards from the dummy and send him. As soon as he is picking up three dummies from one lane with no trouble, leave him as before at X. Walk to the end of C, call 'Mark', drop a dummy on the mown area and do the same at E. Return to your boy, line him up as usual, first on C, and send him. He could start straight, but then veer towards E. This is the dummy foremost in his mind, being the last dropped. Should this happen, this is another time to rush out roaring; don't let him get that dummy he wants so much! When you've stopped him, quieten down, take him back to X and again send him for C. Make him pick it up, even if you have to take him nearly up to it. Then go back to X and get the one from E. He'll quickly learn; this is after all only another version of hand signals.

When you can send him straight down any of the lanes, take the next step. Go down a strip and carry on a couple of yards into the rough grass. Keep your back to your pup and drop a dummy so he cannot see it. Come back up the path and drop one that he does see. Let him retrieve this and then line him up in the direction of the unseen one. As he is used, by now, to going to the end of the path, you shouldn't have any trouble. If he starts to go left or right, stop him and push him back. Once he's picked one or two out of the rough, he'll quickly learn to run straight on beyond the strips. When this stage is reached, you can put out dummies before a training session and go further and further back from the end of the runs. As soon as he is in the area, 'pip' him up and give the command 'Hi lost, seek'. Once he has become used to this command, when he is in an area stop using 'Hi lost' and just use the command, 'Seek' will become the command when he's in the area and has to stay around that particular spot and hunt.

If you haven't got a grid, you can quite easily achieve the same results in a field. In fact, when your puppy has really got the idea and is racing off down the paths and on as required, it is a good thing to start changing your training ground. If he is going well, don't get slack about lining him up and clearly signalling which line to follow. From now on, it's all a matter of practice and working in one or two straight runs each session.

Having been on the subject of lines, we now move on to another form of line, taking a line – that is, following the scent of a wounded bird or rabbit. As already imitated, a dog is remarkably well endowed with olfactory powers; it is no problem for a puppy to follow the trail of his boss. However, that is not what is required and care must be taken in this exercise so that when laying a line you do not leave your own scent for your puppy to follow. The easiest way to avoid this is to recruit an assistant. Take a length of cord or string, your check-cord will do, and attach your drag, which can be a piece of rag or sacking, halfway along it. Keeping the two ends of the cord in your hand, toss the drag forward on to fresh ground, by which I mean an area where you and your helper have not been walking around. Then, each taking one end of the cord, move as far out to the side as you can walk forwards, pulling the drag along the ground between you. Don't go far; fifteen to twenty yards will be ample the first time. When you have gone far enough, move on and round behind the drag before going back, lifting it and dropping a dummy. This exercise is best started on grass just long enough to hide the quarry at the end of the line. Just a reminder in case you've forgotten: make sure your puppy will be working into the wind, so the scent will be blowing towards him. If you happen to be a fisherman and have a good, strong spinning rod, you can cast your drag and reel it in. Cast downwind, so that when you send your puppy from beyond the fall he will be working into the wind enabling him to pick up the scent.

I'm sure you are wondering what to scent the drag with. Those who are in a position to do so often use a pheasant or a rabbit, but not everyone has easy access to those. You can use the artificial pheasant scent which I have already mentioned; it's not bad but it is costly for this purpose. A gamekeeper who taught me much that I learned about dogs in my youth used to use aniseed; one didn't need the scenting powers of a dog to follow the line! That was considered unorthodox by some of his contemporaries, but his argument was that, at this stage, all he was interested in was teaching his puppy to take a line. Having learned that he would automatically take a blood line when he eventually started on the real thing. Whatever you use it is a useful exercise to do, but one I never get too worried about if it does not go as planned. Over the years I have come to the conclusion that the best tutor for taking a line is experience. When a keen young dog has picked a number of hot birds in the shooting field, he will start to work

Ft. Ch. Rossmhor of Clancallum, owned by Mr Malcolm Stringer, winner of 6 Open Stakes and a total of 23 field trial awards.

things out for himself and follow a blood line. Some are quicker than others in learning this, but eventually the penny drops for all. One of the reasons for the variation in progress is that some dogs have a much better nose than others. Weather conditions play an enormous part in how much scent the ground carries or, indeed, how much is discernible by a dog. Many times, in the early part of the season during partridge shooting, when the weather has been hot and dry, I have seen really experienced dogs almost stand on a shot bird and not get as much as a whiff of it. I have seen dogs when, according to the theorists, there should have been no scent, wind a bird when still twenty to thirty yards away from it. Conversely, on days when one would have expected there to be loads of scent, I have seen dog after dog fail for lack of it. In the world of fox hunting much has been written about scent. Many years ago, I hasten to add before the equality of the sexes, one famous Master of Foxhounds summarised the matter as follows, 'There's nothing so queer as scent, except a woman.'

10

Working Tests and the Introduction to Game

All your hard work has been leading towards one goal, whether your interest is in Working Tests, in producing a first-class gundog whom you can shoot over and use for picking up or in the ultimate, Field Trialling. Whichever is your choice – it could be all four – the end result remains the same, a competent, biddable and well-mannered dog.

Let me hark back to the subject of Training Classes. As I have already said, training classes, in my opinion, truly come into their own once your puppy has the basic knowledge upon which to build. If he has passed the O-level stage, then attending classes will be advantageous, but he should not attend more than once a week. That will give you the opportunity to utilise the knowledge that you and your puppy have acquired. Attending classes will get him used to working in the company of other dogs, which is most important. He needs to learn patience and to learn that not every retrieve is his. He has to sit, with his bottom firmly on the ground, whilst other dogs are racing round hunting and retrieving. When you join a class, make sure that you are in a section dealing with work that you have already done. The class then becomes an opportunity for revision. You must, of course, fit in with the general curriculum, but don't allow yourself to be rushed into some exercise for which neither you nor your puppy are yet ready. If you have to go back to doing some kindergarten stuff, don't worry, you're achieving what you want – working your puppy in company. Even if you think it's kid stuff, go along with it and it's almost a certainty that you'll learn something. Everyone has their own methods of training and undoubtedly you'll get some fresh ideas. Anyway, think how bright you and your boy will appear if you go back to elementaries!

Don't get big ideas: you are still very much a novice and there are plenty of pitfalls ahead, you may be heading for one faster than you realise. When you take your lad and work him in company he will undoubtedly get keyed up, it's all very exciting for him. The chances are that he will not react to your commands, at least for the first few sessions, with the alacrity that he does at home, but this is not the pitfall I was talking about. What you must be watchful for is whining. It is the most heinous of sins, and an eliminating fault in a Field Trial and even when trying for a Show Gundog Working Certificate. At the first sign of a squeak, and I really do mean the first one, grab him tightly round the muzzle and give him a good shaking and a sharp 'No'. Make him realise that puppies may be seen but must never be heard. If the whine is the result of pent-up excitement, you have a reasonable chance of stopping him providing you get in there quickly and make your feelings known. If, however, it is inherited, which it can be, you haven't a lot of hope of stopping it, but it's worth having a go. Should it be an inherited trait, then there is more than a good chance that he will have shown this weakness long before you have had him in company. Just sitting waiting to be sent for a dummy can be quite enough to start a puppy off if it has this inherent failing. Whilst on this subject, never allow unnecessary noise – barking or howling. One bad habit can lead to another and, in any case, it is much pleasanter for others not to have a noisy dog around.

One of the first things you will almost certainly be asked to do at a training class will be walking up in line. That means four or six of you, with your dogs off the lead, will be spaced about fifteen to twenty feet apart to walk in line across a field. A dummy will be thrown and a named handler will be told to send his or her dog, whilst the others remain sitting. Possibly a dummy launcher will be used; at this stage it is all good practice. By now your pup knows that he doesn't go until he's told to, or he should know if you've done your job properly, but beware! It's one thing working on your own at home with no distractions, and another when you are in company. So, watch that he doesn't run in. If he does, don't stand around looking helpless; you know what to do. Get out after him. You should be ready for any such happening and be about one-hundredth of a second behind him! Let him think all the devils in hell are after him, scare the living daylights out of him, put him on a lead and yank him back to where he should be. Don't feel self-conscious if you have to do this; this is the sort of thing training classes are for. Don't wait to be told to get after him by whoever is taking the class. If you do that the chances are that your puppy will have passed out of the zone where you can immediately dominate him by then. So keep awake! A sudden movement by you could be enough to make a really keen and over-zealous pup run in – something like taking a swipe at a fly that's bothering you just at the moment the dummy is thrown – these things can easily happen.

I well remember running a very keen young dog in a trial. He was the next dog to go. I was on his right and the judge was close up on his left. A bird went forward, was hit but carried on and suddenly collapsed about a hundred yards in front of the line. My dog marked it and at the same time the judge swung up his arm and, pointing, exclaimed, 'It's down'. The forward movement of the arm and the exclamation right by my dog were enough to make him jump forward a couple of yards. He stopped at the first 'pip' on the whistle, but the damage was done. It was an Open Stake, so the judge who was the cause of the trouble told me to put him on the lead and take him out. Such are the tribulations of Trialling, and this is a good example of how a tensed-up keen young dog can react to some sudden movement. Having said all this, if you are watchful, the chances are that your boy will not fall from grace.

Winning English Team at Int. Gundog Obedience Competition, Dublin 1975. L to r: J. Clitheroe, Bee of Bedingham Hall, E. Baldwin, Palgrave Swinbrook Fern, M. Twist, Bryanstown Seamus, (Seamus won BOB Cardiff Ch Show 1974). (Photo East Anglian Daily Times).

If he does, at a training class you can bring home to him the error of his ways. You cannot do that at a Working Test or Field Trial.

How do you get in touch with a club running training classes? There are numerous clubs organising these throughout the country and a little judicious enquiring around your area should bring you an answer. If not, contact the United Retriever Club, which have a lot of area branches (addresses available from the KC). Alternatively, your local Golden Retriever Club may be able to put you in touch with a club that does.

Even if you are going to classes, keep plugging away at home. Try all the time to improve the quality of your pup's work, varying his retrieves as much as possible. I always remember Lady Hill-Wood, a most knowledgeable and senior Field Trial judge, when judging at the Irish Retriever Championship Field Trial, telling me that she always kept a couple of dummies in her car. As she was motoring through the country, if she saw what would be a testing and possibly unusual retrieve, she would stop and work her dog(s), providing she had the time. I thought this showed good sense and for many years took a leaf out of her book. These days it might not be quite so easy; there is not the freedom in the countryside that there used to be. Farmers have become far more aggressive towards trespassers on their land. One can't really blame them with all the vandalism with which they are so frequently faced these days. However, if you were tempted and were caught, the worst that could happen would be a right rollicking from an irate landowner! If you are not of a daring nature, there are still a lot of commons and forestry and moorland areas where you can give your pup some interesting and varied work and it's worth keeping the possibilities in mind.

Working Tests are a natural progression from what you have been doing over the past months. There will be those who have no desire to go beyond this point except, possibly, to attain their Show Gundog Working Certificate. Tests can be most enjoyable and highly competitive, but they cannot be compared with field trials for assessing a dog's true ability. However, if this is what you think you want to do, fair enough. It is my belief that any work for a gundog is better than no work; it all makes his life that much more interesting. Tests are usually run by breed clubs, by those catering for field trials and by the United Retriever Club, which I have already mentioned. If you have any problems in finding out what clubs there are in your area, you can always enquire of the Kennel Club. You should, however, ask about field trial clubs, not working test ones. At present, tests are not licensed by the Kennel Club. In working gundog circles they are looked upon as a form of advanced training. As a result, the promoting body make their own rules and conditions. This state of affairs suits everyone admirably. However, at the time of writing, the Kennel Club are trying to get in on the act, to introduce screeds of rules and regulations. Inevitably, if they succeed, and eventually they will, it will mean that tests will have to be licensed and will be subject to Kennel Club control. If this happens, it is my belief that this will eventually lead to yet another division within the gundog breeds and the introduction of yet another title, that of Working Test Champion. That would give five possible titles within breeds that were originally evolved for one purpose – to produce working gundogs. For those not *au fait* with the current situation, one can already acquire the following titles: Champion, Field Trial Champion, Show Champion and Obedience Champion.

Let us return to tests and what you are likely to be asked to do in one confined to Puppies and Non-Winners. There will be almost certainly four exercises. The first is likely to be a walk-up in line, with an unseen retrieve behind the line and a mark forward, retrieving the former first. Alternatively, you may find two dummies are thrown forward, one right and one left, and you will be expected to pick them in whatever order the judge decides. The second exercise could be a mark into cover, possibly over a fence or ditch. The third will probably be a water test, a seen retrieve from or across water. Finally, there will be an unseen one from cover, with quite a distance of open ground to cross first. There is nothing too difficult in any of that and, if your training has gone well, your puppy should be well able to do it. Open Tests are a progression from what I have described, with, obviously, more difficult things to be achieved, like sending your dog eighty to a hundred yards across water for an unseen retrieve on the far bank, or even quite a distance out in the field beyond it. There could be various diversions as your dog is going out or coming back, or a simulated drive. The latter involves three or four guns all firing away, whilst dummies positively rain down around the dogs. This, of course, is to test your dog's steadiness.

On the basis of one thing leading to another, the next logical move forward is Cold Game Tests, These are tests where cold game, usually pigeons, are used instead of dummies. Pigeons, of course, are not game in the accepted sense of the word, but it would become a somewhat costly operation these days if pheasants and partridges were used.

This brings us to the next sequence in the training programme, an important exercise whichever road you are following, the introduction to cold game. Most people start with a pigeon. Let your puppy sniff it, but watch out that he doesn't make a grab at it. When he is sufficiently aroused and really showing interest in this new experience, put the pigeon in an old sock or nylon stocking. Let him take it in his mouth, but be careful that he doesn't bite it; be ready to slip your finger over his bottom lip and press down if you think he is starting to hold it a bit too tightly. If there is no problem, throw it for him. Make sure it lands in a bit of rough grass or light cover so that he cannot see it and has to use his nose. If it is on bare ground where it can be seen easily, there is a risk that he will 'hit' it too hard if he is really keen, and damage it. When he is retrieving satisfactorily, move on to the next stage, not necessarily on the same day.

The next stage is a cold bird, not in a sock. It is possible that all you can get is a wood pigeon. They have one big disadvantage: their feathers come out extremely easily. This could result in your puppy having a mouthful of loose feathers which he will not enjoy and might even put him off retrieving birds. If you do have to use a wood pigeon, then make it one bird for one retrieve! Further, tuck the head under a wing and put an elastic band tightly around it. By doing this you cover much of the body with the wing feathers, and these do not come out as easily as those on the breast and back. You will also prevent the puppy retrieving the pigeon by it's head only. If you can obtain some Blue Rocks, a species of wild pigeon quite common in some areas, so much the better; their feathers do not come out like those of a wood pigeon. Should you, through necessity, have to use a wood pigeon, as soon as you have received the bird from your puppy clear any feathers out of his mouth.

A little forethought with regard to your game requirements during the shooting season can save you a lot of trouble. Most people these days have a freezer; if you have one you can acquire some pigeons and hen pheasants during the season whilst they are plentiful. Where do you get them? One source is local shoots. Then many country towns have weekly street markets where game is sold, or you can look up game dealers in the *Yellow Pages*. You can, of course, go to the top of the market and go to a poulterer. If you do, don't do as a friend of mine did. She went into the shop and bought two hen pheasants to start her puppy retrieving game. As she had quite a lot to do in town, she said she would collect them in a couple of hours' time, on her way back to the car. When she returned, she was greeted by a smiling shop assistant, who said, 'Your pheasants are ready, madam. As I had some time to spare, I've plucked and dressed them for you; there will be no extra charge!' Faced with what these days was very unusual service, my friend hadn't the heart to say anything. You will have noted that I said 'hens'. The reason for this is that they are smaller and lighter than cock birds and, therefore, easier for a puppy to carry. Whilst on the subject of obtaining game, I have often been asked, 'Where can I get a pheasant and how much will it cost?' This has usually been a question put by someone anxious to put their dog in for a Show Gundog Working Certificate. I have given the required information regarding the sources and have told them that currently a brace from a shoot will cost £2.50 to £3 at the most and, probably, that each bird from a poulterer will cost that much. Frequently the reply has been, 'Oh, that's a bit expensive.' The same person will, without hesitation, spend up to £18 on entering their dog in one class at a Championship Show, plus petrol to get there, and think nothing of it!

Once your pup is retrieving from the open, then start working him on cold birds from cover. This will get him using his nose to find game and give him experience in carrying it through undergrowth. A pheasant is nothing like as easy for a puppy to carry as a dummy. If you are fortunate enough to have some pheasants, don't use them more than two or three times at the most, and preferably only once. However, I do appreciate the problem of supply, which means that you will want to get the most from your birds. The trouble is that when they've been used several times they become wet, from saliva, across the back. It is here that a dog normally picks up a bird and when the feathers are wet they become distasteful. When this happens your puppy will almost certainly start to mouth it, that is, pick it up, put it down and generally mess around. He's had enough of this soggy object and has no further desire to carry it. Because of this, if you force him he could well grip it too firmly and this could easily lead to his developing a hard mouth. One well-executed retrieve with a fresh pheasant is of far greater value than several mediocre ones with a wet and bedraggled bird.

The next move forward is retrieving freshly shot game that is still warm. This is very exciting for your puppy; apart from there being more scent with a warm bird, there will be a blood scent, something that he has not experienced before. For you, particularly if it is the first time, this will be an anxious moment, to say the least! Whilst you must be near the gun, don't get too close so that there is a risk of it being fired directly over your boy's head; even some experienced dogs are not too keen on that. If you have ever stood immediately behind a gun (in this case meaning the person doing the shooting) and the latter has swung round and fired directly above your head, you'll understand why! There has been more than one person whose eardrum has been perforated in this fashion. That is why these days the majority of guns use earplugs and, indeed, that is a wise thing to do if you are standing in a line when working your dog. Before sending your puppy for whatever has been shot, make certain that it is dead and motionless. Do not send your puppy for a wounded bird. That could be inviting trouble. If it moves, there is a great temptation for any puppy to grab it and, indeed, to bite it. Try to avoid this if you possibly can. Having said this, let me add that you should not get too alarmed if he is a bit rough with his first few warm birds; that is by no means unusual. Ideally, a quick pick-up and a fast return is what is required. A puppy, on his first encounter with a freshly shot bird, will possibly lift it and put it down several times before getting a sufficiently good hold to retrieve it. The lighter his mouth the more likely this is to happen, but watch carefully and if there is the slightest suspicion that he is biting it get out to him at once. It is quite likely that your pup will lift the bird by the wing and, head held high, come galloping back, probably dropping it several times en route. This is nothing to worry about; as yet he doesn't know how to pick a bird correctly. When I first take a puppy out to shoot over, I put a couple of strong elastic bands in my pocket. Should he bring a bird back by the wing, I put a band round it. Sit him down and walk forward, placing the bird on the ground. It should be breast down so that he automatically picks it up across the back when sent. As soon as you take the bird from him, examine it to see that it has not been damaged. You do this by laying it on its back in the palm of your hand and feeling the ribcage. If this is intact, all is well. A hard-mouthed dog will crush the ribs, and that is an eliminating fault in any test involving game. There is normally no cure, although on two occasions I have been able to achieve one. Both successes were with young dogs that had run with a modicum of success in trials. Both were sent for wounded birds, cock pheasants, and one dog was spurred andthe other pecked; in each case I saw it happen. Both dogs were laid open to the bone, one between the eyes and the other on the lower jaw. The next few birds they picked were given no chance either to spur or peck! However, I got them over their problem. The cure is pretty drastic and like forced retrieving is not something to be undertaken by a beginner. If you should be unfortunate enough to have a puppy with a hard mouth, then his future, as far as competition is concerned, lies in Working Tests and the Show Ring, not in Field Trials. However, take heart, Goldens normally have very soft mouths.

It may have occurred to readers that I have not suggested using rabbits as cold game. Some people do, but I feel that is asking for trouble. It will be time enough to introduce your puppy to fur when he is retrieving feather without any problems. Rabbits are extremely attractive to our young canine friends and a great source of temptation. There is a KC rule that a puppy need not pick fur in a field trial. This is good, but in the forty years that I have been judging at trials, I have only once heard this rule invoked. How do you start making your puppy steady to fur? Again, much depends on circumstances. The ideal way is in a rabbit pen, an enclosed area with rabbits running around in it, with, I should add, plenty of escape pipes, arcs and stick heaps. If you can find such facilities – and many professional trainers have them – try to get permission to use it. If you are successful, take your pup in on a lead and choke-chain. Walk around with him. As soon as you put up a rabbit and it runs off, give a hard jerk on the chain and a sharp 'No'. When he ceases to pay any attention to the rab-bits, which will be very quickly in most cases, take him in on a check-cord. Throw a dummy to within a few feet of a rabbit and send your pup. Keep the cord running out through your hand, so that you can bring him up short should he decide to have a go for the rabbit instead of the dummy. If this happens, get out to him, give him a good shake and a real telling-off and start again. He will quickly realise that the best policy is to turn a blind eye to these little furry creatures. When he is totally ignoring them, put out a couple of blinds in the pen and send your puppy for them, but be on your toes. If he as much as looks at a rabbit give a shout, and be ready to get in there quickly should the occasion arise. The owners of rabbit pens do not take kindly to the inmates being chopped; it could be expensive too! Should you be fortunate enough to obtain the use of these facilities, a token of appreciation in the form of a bottle of the owner's favourite tipple would not come amiss.

It is, of course, possible to make your own rabbit pen, but that is costly and a lot of work for one puppy. However, what you should do depends on what your ultimate goal happens to be. Should you be planning to enter the world of field trialling, then steadiness to fur is a must. Before the advent of myxomatosis the rabbit population was such that steadying a puppy was no great problem. Finding reasonable numbers in the wild for this purpose might be difficult now, but it is not impossible. Once your puppy has learned not to think even about chasing either hares or rabbits, then it is time to let him start retrieving dead ones. Finally, before taking your puppy off for a real day's work, as opposed to picking a warm bird or two under the closest supervision, try to make sure that he knows that sheep are 100 per cent taboo! How easy this is to achieve entirely depends on whether you live in an area with a high number of sheep. The same principles apply as in training your puppy not to chase fur.

Shannon

Dedicated to
Irish Champion Bryanstown Shannon of Yeo

Farewell Shannon! The trees do sigh;
Proud and noble till you went away,
To game-filled halcyon coverts – not to die,
But hunt, as oft you did, the live-long day.
Seeking out your quarry, however hard it ran,
Proud gundog excelsior, farewell Shan!

Farewell Friend! The rippling rivers cry;
What joy you gave and memories left
Of wondrous days spent 'neath the wintry sky.
Of high cocks shot, retrieved with skill so deft;
No cover so thick that you could not it rend,
Returning quickly game to outstretched hand.
Farewell Friend!

Farewell Shannon! Nor'east winds do whisper;
How oft they whipped your golden coat
Awaiting morn's light – the geese and ducks to stir,
As patiently you sat in reed enshrouded boat,
Alert, expectant, marking where the shot birds fell;
Man could have no greater friend. Shannon farewell!

Michael F. Twist

105

11

Shooting and Picking up

That's it then, you have a trained gundog. Really it's a bit like having passed your driving test: you have the theory and the basic ability, and from now on it's a question of gaining experience. The latter can only be acquired in the field. This means shooting over your puppy. If you own a gun and have somewhere to use it, no problem. If, on the other hand, you have a gun and can shoot but have nowhere to go, it leaves you in a bit of a quandary. However, you might solve this by keeping an eye on the shooting and/or sporting columns in your local paper or in the *Shooting Times*. There is often pigeon and rabbit shooting advertised at quite reasonable prices – at least, reasonable when compared with the cost of some other sports. I have known people so bitten by the dog training bug that they have taken up shooting. If you are moved to do this, then, for goodness sake, go to a shooting school first. Learn not only to shoot properly but, much more important, what the correct safety procedures are. Once you can shoot and are safe, it could well pay you to join a gun club or association.

Shooting can be divided into several categories. In one of these you yourself do not have to shoot but you find a contact who does. If you are not actually shooting, it will enable you to continue your puppy's education. However, before embarking on this, you must decide what your ultimate objective is. Is it to have fun with and provide fun for your dog, to obtain your Show Gundog Working Certificate or to do picking up or field trialling? To the novice, work is probably just work. To some extent that is true but the type of work you ask your puppy to do can effect his biddability and steadiness. For example, you might meet someone with a rough shoot who likes to have a walk round with his gun and dog looking for something for the pot. If you were invited along, the chances are that you would be asked to use your lad to hunt for and flush game. A Golden is perfectly capable of doing this, although, normally, such work would be the lot of a spaniel. This is excellent experience if all you want is to enjoy your dog and develop his natural instincts, and possibly to obtain his Show Gundog Working Certificate. However, if

Oriule Drummer Boy (Sire Ch Bryanstown Gaucho, dam Golden Amanda of Oriule). Winner of 29 field trial awards, first prizewinner at Championship Shows, BOB winner at Open Shows. Owner Mr P. Watts. Breeder Mrs H. Watts (Photo by Graham Cox).

you are considering serious picking up, or running him in a Field Trial, then this is not for you. Incidentally, if this is all that you want to do, then you don't really need to work through the A-level stage, but there is one exception: your pup must master stopping on the whistle. You don't want him ranging so far in front that the game he puts up is out of shot! There should be no problem in getting him to do this. You've taught him to go out and hunt and he knows the stop and recall whistle.

Possibly your interest is wildfowling; you may have a love for the solitude of the marshes and mudflats. Goldens, I know from many years of experience, are ideal for this and are wonderful companions. It takes a really good gundog to excel in this sphere. He has to be brave and biddable and to be able to take hand signals both on land and in water. It was wildfowling that first got me interested in training dogs up to field trial standards. Many good gundogs will swim a river and hunt the rushes on the far side, but that is their limit. On one shoot in which I had an interest in Ireland, there were two rivers on which we regularly did a morning flight. Invariably when it was light enough and the shooting was over, one could see duck lying out on the grassland, often fifty or a hundred yards beyond the bank. The dogs that I and my friends had would make the long swim across the often fast flowing river and hunt and retrieve anything from the rushes on the far side, but they would not go out and hunt the callows beyond. This was because they had never been trained to take hand signals when at a distance. If it is your aim to shoot in these conditions then advance training will be a great help.

In your search to find work for your dog, you may make contact with someone in a small shoot, the kind where they supplement the wild stock by putting down a couple of hundred reared birds and an average day is around forty head. Such shoots are usually keepered by one of the syndicate and, normally, great fun days. The participants, divided into two groups and ably assisted by wives and girl-friends, alternating as standing forward guns and walking guns-cum-beaters. If you take part, you will almost certainly find yourself walking all the time and you will be expected to hunt your dog as well as to use him to retrieve.

Finally, much the most common kind of shoot is the properly keepered one, mostly with reared birds, although there are a number of excellent large shoots that rely entirely on wild stock. It is at a shoot in this category that the non-shooting reader is most likely to find an opportunity to work his/her dog. How do you set about achieving this? It's not easy but, if you are really keen, it is most

Ch Standerwick Thomasina (Sire FT Ch Holway Spinner, dam Strathcarron Seil of Standerwick). The only purely field trial bred Golden to attain the title Champion. Winner of 4 CCs and 11 Field Trial awards. Owners/Breeders Miss J. Gill and Mrs D. Philpott. (Photo by Graham Cox).

certainly not impossible. First, you have to locate a shoot. This should not be difficult in a country area. The local pub is often a fund of information regarding such matters. Having found a shoot, then you have to make contact with the owner or, probably better still, the head gamekeeper. These days running a big shoot is a very costly business. To start with, there are the beaters, the people who, under the control of the gamekeeper, walk through woods, fields and moors, driving the game forward and over the waiting guns. This army of often thirty-five or more people have to be paid, and according to the area, the rate can vary from £15 to £20 a day with, frequently, free beer at lunch-time. Pickers-up, whose job it is to be back behind the guns collecting wounded game or, indeed, any that cannot be picked by hand, normally receive slightly more than that and also a brace of birds. Others take part in that task for nothing, finding a day out in the country with their dog ample reward.

When you have located a gamekeeper, go and see him. Explain that you have a young dog which is trained as far as you can go without further experience out shooting. Offer your services as a beater, free, providing you can bring your dog. Emphasise that, until you were told otherwise, you would keep him on a lead. You might receive a rebuff at your first attempt, but don't be put off. Most gamekeepers are extremely nice people and, when time permits, they are usually willing to help those interested in shooting and country pursuits. Once you can get your foot in the door you should be away, but don't try to rush things. For the first time or two that you are out, be content to be a beater; watch, learn and teach. You have trained your puppy not to pick up diversionary dummies and to ignore rabbits; now is your chance to instil in him the knowledge that live unshot game are not for chasing. Have him on a choke-chain and a short check-cord. Keep telling him 'No' as pheasants run in front of you. If he makes any attempt to go after them, bring him up short and let him know that such behaviour is taboo! Should you become friendly with the keeper, he might, on a non-shooting day, let you

FT Ch Volvo of Palgrave (Sire Belway Vanguard, dam Hilost Peril). 2nd in The Retriever Championship 1978.

bring your lad along to accompany him around the shoot; that will give you ample opportunity to emphasis to your boy that he must not chase. If you are confident that your lad won't run in, ask if you can slip him off the lead during the early part of a drive, that is, before there is too big a concentration of birds running around in front of him. Even if you are not told to do so, put him back on the lead as you get towards the end of the drive. It is better to be safe than sorry.

When you are on reasonably good terms with the keeper, ask him if, at the end of the drive, you can let your boy pick a bird. The answer will almost certainly be 'Yes'. The birds have to be picked and taken to the game-cart, so why shouldn't you be in on the act? However, be careful, don't send your pup for a bird that someone else is already working a dog on and don't get into the general mêlée of guns' and beaters' dogs 'hoovering' indiscriminately. Find a bird away on its own where your pup will have a chance to concentrate on what he is doing. To begin with, one bird a drive will be just fine. It will not be long before, at the end of a drive, a bird that has started to go forward turns, is shot and falls back in the wood from which the beaters have just come. If you happen to be close to the keeper – and you would be wise to see that you are – offer to go back, and look for it. If you receive agreement, this is your big chance; don't fail! Should you be successful, without making too much of a song and dance about it make sure the keeper knows you got it. The chances are that you'll be sent on a similar mission. In fact, it's a case of one good retrieve leads to another!

The day should come when, on reporting for beater duty, you'll be told that they, the shoot, are short of a picker-up and you will find yourself promoted for the day. This is the chance you've been waiting for. The regulars will be experienced; it is quite likely that one or more could be a professional trainer and field trialler of some note. Without being too subservient, explain that it is your first day picking-up and ask to be told where to go and what to do. Whatever you do, if you are certain there is a wounded bird down and your dog can't find it, don't just walk off and leave it. Tell your companions and ask them to try for it; after all, your boy is still very inexperienced. On some shoots instructions are given to the pickers-up by the owner or the head of the shooting syndicate for each drive. On others, where there is a regular team, the pickers-up receive a list of the drives and are left to get on with it. Normally the shoot provides transport so they are entirely independent. Your main job will be picking birds that fall away back

111

behind the line of guns, many of which the guns may well not know they've even hit.

I remember once, many years ago, on a shoot where I have picked up for nearly twenty seasons, being told to go to place some four to five hundred yards behind the guns. My appointed spot was on the banks of a small stream which had a few yards of hazel and scrub on either side. I did not think the prospects of work were very great; the only hope was that there was a strong and wind blowing straight from the guns. The pheasants would be coming over them high and fast. I had two very experienced dogs with me, both Open Stake winners. I stationed myself some ten yards out from the stream on some plough.

I was in full view of any birds coming my way and I could see several hundred yards in either direction along the stream. Shooting began and it was not many minutes before a cock, apparently unharmed, came up the little valley where I stood. It suddenly pitched in about twenty yards beyond me. As it had been chivvied by beaters and almost certainly shot at, this seemed an odd thing to do. I knew the pheasant must have seen me, so I sent a dog. He was back, almost immediately, with the cock which was now quite dead. Nine more pheasants landed by the stream and many more carried on far beyond me. Some of those that landed dropped in as much as a hundred yards before they reached me, some nearly as far beyond me. Each time I sent a dog. Seven were dead birds and two were runners. When I rejoined the rest of the party, having first been to the game-cart, the owner asked me if I had picked up the cock that had been hit and come my way. When I replied that I had and that I had picked up nine others, he could hardly believe it. This illustrates the importance of pickers-up being well back behind the guns on such a day.

To return to your first day as a picker-up, at each drive you will be told the area that is your responsibility. Position yourself so that you can see as much as possible and watch carefully. Mark and remember any birds which you think have been hit. According to the rules of the shoot, you may have to wait until the end of the drive before trying for a bird, or you may be allowed, indeed encouraged, to send your dog as soon as a bird is down. Personally, I am in favour of the latter, with three provisos: first, that by working your dog you are not turning the birds and stopping them from going over the guns; secondly, that you are in no way distracting the guns; and, thirdly, that you can work your dog without leaving your vantage point. If you leave your position, whilst you are off chasing one bird you may well miss marking a number of others.

Subject to these three conditions, I am in favour of picking birds as they fall. After more than fifty years of picking up and shooting, I am convinced that more game is lost by waiting until the drive is over than if you pick it as it comes down.

You may be fortunate and find that one of your companions for the day is a professional of some note in the field trialling world or, possibly, one of the top amateurs. If you have this luck, don't be afraid to ask questions and, above all, watch! See how he, or indeed she, handles his/her dog and how the dog responds. Then compare it with your young fellow. That will give you some idea about how much more both of you have to learn, but don't get despondent if there seems to be a vast difference. Aim high. The chances are that the super handler you are watching with admiration and not a little envy was no better than you with his/her first dog!

Now for a few do's and dont's when you are picking-up. There will be times when you are told to go and stand with the guns. You may not be assigned to a specific gun; if you are not, don't attach yourself to one who has a dog. When you are walking out to take your places in the line, walk behind the guns, NOT IN FRONT. Having taken up your position, be friendly and chat if the gun seems inclined to, but stop as soon as game starts to show. Once that happens, unless told to do otherwise, remain right behind the gun, keep quiet and crouch down out of the way.

Never send your dog for a bird when someone else is already trying a dog for it. Many of the leading field triallers do much of their training whilst picking-up and do not take kindly to someone – particularly a beginner – coming in on a bird they are already working for.

Never claim to have found a bird unless you have. There is no disgrace in failing; no dog is infallible. A great friend of mine had a habit, when there was a new professional, paid picker-up out on his shoot for the first time, of saying that he had a bird down in a certain place and sending the new recruit for it. Later he would enquire if the latter had found it. If the answer was in the affirmative we seldom saw that person again, for the simple reason that there was no bird down in the first place!

Never pick birds within the orbit of a gun who has his own dog. He doesn't bring it with him to sit patiently through a drive and then find you've picked everything he has shot. Many guns get as much pleasure from working their dogs as they do from shooting. I well remember some years ago, on a shoot where I regularly picked up, our ranks being swollen by a new member of the team, whom I will call X. One of the guns, a good friend of mine and a keen dog man, had recently purchased a top-class dog at considerable expense. Halfway through the morning we did a drive in which, for some ten years, I had gone back some three to four hundred yards behind the line of guns to a small area of open woodland. I asked the owner if I should go to my usual place and was told not to as he was putting X there. I was to go out on the flank. I knew it was most unlikely that I would have anything to do, but it was a lovely sunny morning and I would have a great view of everything that was happening. The guns went to their position, my friend sitting his new acquisition well out in front of him. I saw X heading for the wood. Then, to my horror, I saw the new picker-up settle into a ditch by the remains of an old hedge that crossed the field, not more than eighty to a hundred yards behind the guns. The stubble was long and it would be impossible to see any birds once they hit the ground. It was not long before my friend, a brilliant shot, dropped the first bird, which fell not more than thirty yards from the ditch. After a minute up popped X, sent a dog, retrieved the bird and again disappeared from sight. This happened four times before the drive was over. When it was, I headed back to the guns. My friend, having put his gun away,

Mr & Mrs R. Rains Ch Millgreen Magum winner of 11 CCs and 10 BOBs. Although featured in his 'show clothes', he regularly picks up during the shooting season.

called up his dog and started to work it, with no result! I was about twenty yards away from him when X appeared out of the ditch carrying five pheasants and enquiring if they were the ones my friend was looking for. The roar was frightening. I thought my friend was going to have a fit! His, language was magnificent and the fact that there were ladies present in no way curbed his rancour – his face was scarlet with fury and remained so for some minutes. So, NEVER, NEVER pick a gun's birds if he has a dog, unless specifically asked to do so by him or instructed by whoever is running the shoot.

Once you have established yourself as a competent picker-up you will, in most areas, have little difficulty in getting all the work you want and the road to field trialling will be open to you.

Ir Ch Bryanstown Shannon of Yeo (at 16 months, before he got his title) winner of 14 Ft. awards including one 1st & three 2nds in AV Open Stakes, together with Bryanstown Camrose Gale, 9 Ft awards including 1st AV Open Stake and Ir Ch Bryanstown Diplomat of Ulvin winner of 9 Ft awards. Photo taken on an evening out training. The bag was 52, shot in 1 hr & 10 mins.

Tara

Dedicated to
Irish Champion Bryanstown Camrose Gail

As she lies by the fire with a sigh and a twitch,
I'm talking of Tara, my old Golden bitch.
I think of the days when she still galloped free
And walked marshes and fields, with her head by
my knee.

She was made up a Champion before being two,
That in itself is a feat claimed by few!
A nature so kind, she would give of her all,
Be it getting a runner, or playing at ball.

Her first Open Stake I still well remember,
It was cold, it was wet, it was late in December.
There were four of us left for the judges to place,
As I stood near the lake with the rain in my face.

A woodcock flew high, by the wind it was caught,
The first gun his barrels he emptied for naught.
The second, a hit, but not a clean kill
And that cock was in water before it lay still.

'Number three, send your dog a soon as you're ready.'
I glanced down at Tara, making sure she was steady,
Being glad at this time we were last on the card,
For whoever got this it was bound to be hard.

Two gun shots of scrub before lake-fringing reed,
Where in summer the duck and the little grebe breed;
Then twenty yards more to clear open water,
I know I for one wished the distance were shorter.

Number three was called in and five was now trying
Through brambles and scrub and nettles still dying.
The cover's too thick, the distance too great,
And now it's the chance of the next – number eight.

The cock's drifting further – the story the same,
The handler exhorting his dog by it's name.
'Call him in' says the judge as he looks round at me.
'Go quick, number twelve – if the cock you still see.'

It's two hundred yards or more to the mark.
Light is quick fading, an' soon't will be dark.
A click of the fingers, 'Hi lost' and 'get back'.
This is no time for work that is slack.

Tara's out through the cover and into the reed,
This is a time for the luck we all need,
A wait like forever – why won't she appear?
Ah! There she is now in the lake, swimming clear.

She's on the right line, twenty yards more to go
An' the steward, all smiles, says, 'I think it will snow.'
I heard him quite vaguely but gave not a jot,
As I realised with joy that woodcock she'd got.

That stake won so memorably, how years seem to fly,
Season 'pon season have all drifted by,
Now Tara lies whuffling, all twitches and smiles
As she dreams of some runner she's chasing for miles.

What pleasures dogs give us, what joy and what fun,
By fireside, in show ring, in field with the gun,
Just marred by that factor of seven to one.
If *only* our years could concurrently run!

                                        Michael F. Twist

FT Ch Treunair Cala (Sire Treunair Ciabhach or Treunair Lunga, dam Gay Vandra).
Winner of IGL Retriever Championship 1952.
Owner/Breeder Miss E. J. C. Train (Mrs J. Lumsden).

12

Field Trialling

If you venture into the world of field trialling you be entering the most difficult and, at the same time, most rewarding of the many specialist areas that there now are in the gundog world. To achieve success in this sphere, not only does your dog have to be above average, but also you have to be dedicated. In addition to having dedication, you will require a certain flair and natural affinity in order to reach the top; qualities with which only a few have the good fortune to be endowed. Many can train dogs and train them well, but those such as June Atkinson and Eric Baldwin, to name but two, who have that little extra something are the exception rather than the rule.

There is no similarity between winning a first in the show ring and in the field, quite apart from the fact that one is for beauty and the other for ability. For example, at a Championship Show there are anything from twenty to twenty-four first prizes up for grabs – there could be, according to Kennel Club regulations, as many as thirty-two. At a Field Trial there is one. In a show success depends on the individual likes and dislikes of one judge. In a Trial you have to satisfy a minimum of three judges, frequently four, as to your dog's superiority and claim for top honours on the day. Individual preferences have little or no bearing on the outcome of a trial. Add to this the fact that there are virtually no Kennel Club rules that can lead to elimination in the show ring but there are five rules applicable to trials that can do that, and you will, I think, get the point I am making.

The five eliminating faults are hard mouth, whining, running in and chasing, failing to enter water and being out of control. None of these should be a problem to you IF you have done your training correctly, given your boy sufficient experience in the shooting field and, in your enthusiasm for picking up, not allowed him to get out of control. The latter is very easy to do with a keen, hard-going young dog. Should you fancy your chances in trialling – and it is a fascinating pastime – before actually entering for a trial, go and watch as many as you can. Don't be afraid to ask questions and, if you get the chance to be in the line acting as a steward for one of the judges, carrying a number board or doing some other task, take it. When you have been to several trials you should be in a position to properly assess your pup's ability and trial potential. Don't run him for the sake of running him. A field trial is a competition and should be entered with both the desire and feeling that you can win. Nearly every field trial these days is vastly oversubscribed and a ballot is held to select the few fortunates who will be able to run their dogs. Don't enter your lad until you genuinely think he is ready; otherwise you could easily deprive someone whose dog is more advanced and ready for a trial than yours of a chance to take part. I remember once being with Eric Baldwin when a young enthusiast brought his dog along for Eric's opinion. He also wanted to know when he should enter his dog in a Puppy/Novice Stake. The latter Eric answered for him by saying, 'When you think he's good enough at home to win an Open Stake, then it is time enough to put him in a Novice.' That was sound advice. We have all had what looked like champions at home, but when we have had them out in company at a trial they may have given a quite different impression!

In addition to the eliminating faults already mentioned, there are a number of what are described by the Kennel Club as major faults. They are failing to find game, unsteadiness at heel, disturbing ground, slack and unbusinesslike work, noisy handling, poor control, changing birds and an eye-wipe. I am never quite sure why these are listed separately from the eliminating faults because, with the present-day standards in trials, they lead to elimination as well. The first two really require no explanation. Disturbing ground normally means that a dog is galloping around, away from the area where it is supposed to be hunting, and is putting up game and ignoring his handler. Therefore he is out of control and so, *ipso facto*, the fault becomes an eliminating one. However, the fault can be caused by the judge who, by asking for a retrieve over an excessively long distance, may force the handler into being noisy when trying to get his dog out far enough, thereby disturbing game. Slack work really means that a dog is not hunting properly; such a dog comes in that category I have already mentioned of those that potter out to please and really shouldn't be entered in a field trial. Noisy handling is perhaps a fault that does not warrant elimination; it really depends on the volume. There is a big difference between a handler using his voice to push a dog back on a very difficult retrieve and a handler continually shouting and blowing a whistle. Certainly anyone who does make a lot of unnecessary noise will be very severely marked down, if not actually eliminated. As for poor control, there is only a thin dividing line between this and being out of control and if control is consistently poor throughout a trial it would certainly lead to elimination. Changing birds, as I said earlier, is a cardinal sin; I cannot remember, in the fortyfive to fifty years I have been attending and judging at trials, a dog changing birds and getting an award – that is, when the judges have known it has happened! An eye-wipe, for the benefit of those who are not familiar with this term, is when one or more dogs fail on a retrieve and then it is picked by another. The dog that has picked the bird is said to have eye-wiped the others. The value of such an achievement is entirely dependent on how difficult the retrieve was in the first place and on the quality of the dogs that failed.

So far I have only mentioned those things which lead to trouble and remorse, those that judges do not want to see. What they do want to see is a dog with a good nose and a natural game-finding ability – that is what it is all about. That means a dog needs to hunt within the area that has been indicated by the judges, to have speed and to work with drive and style. He must mark where game falls and be able to go right to the spot without any help from his handler, and must gather it up and return it quickly to hand. The ideal dog is always under control, will answer immediately to the whistle and yet will not be constantly looking for help; further, he will be able to take the line of a runner and will really persevere when doing so. If your lad has most of these qualities and you are a quiet handler, then certainly have a go. Having said all this, however good your boy turns out to be, you will need a modicum of luck. Even the very best, such as a winner of the Retriever Championship, can come to grief on a bad scenting day when he is first dog down on a strong runner. Whilst failure is not specified by the Kennel Club as an eliminating fault, some judges, even very experienced ones, often treat it as such. Many others, like myself, would not discard a dog if it has worked really well, showed drive and perseverance and had failed not through lack of ability but because of atrocious scenting conditions. Nevertheless, once a dog has a mark against his name for a first dog failure, it is a long haul back to a place in the top awards – but it can be done.

There are various categories of trials, starting with that for Novice Dogs/Novice Handlers, which is self-explanatory. Next is the Puppy/Novice category, the title of which is again explicit. Then come Open and All-Aged Stakes, which are qualifying stakes into Qualifying and Non-Qualifying. They are either twenty-four-dog two-day stakes or twelve-dog one-day stakes. Qualifying means that the stake carries a qualification for or towards eligibility to run in the Retriever Championship. A twenty-four-dog stake carries an 'A' qualification for the winner and a 'B' for the second. A twelve-dog stake carries a 'B' qualification. To run in the Championship a dog must have one 'A' or three 'B's. The winner of a Non-Qualifying Stake is not eligible to compete in the Championships. This is not necessarily because the standard of work is inferior, but because field trialling has become so popular that, with the ever-increasing number of stakes, it would be impossible to accommodate all the winners in the championship. I have said that the work is not necessarily inferior, but it would be reasonable to assume that the standard in the qualifying stakes would be higher overall, in view of the fact that all those having dogs that they feel could win the Blue Ribbon of Trialling will be looking for places in these stakes. Finally, there is the Retriever Championship, the mecca for all dedicated field triallers, to compete in which is an honour. To go further and attain an award is a major achievement; to win it is the lot of an élite few. There is no trial in the world where the game-finding ability of a dog is more fully tested.

However, you do not have to reach such heights to derive tremendous pleasure and gratification from trialling and to many with a genuine interest in every aspect of the breed a Certificate of Merit can bring as much satisfaction as does the winning of a major stake to the field trial purist. It is regrettable that over the years a vast division has occurred within the breed, as it has in all gundog breeds, between work and show. Probably the greatest disservice the Kennel Club ever did to the gundog breeds as a whole was the introduction of the Show Champion. Also, if they had, like some other Kennel Clubs, bought in a ruling that to gain the title of Field Trial Champion a dog had to qualify on the bench, then there would not have been the vast difference between the types that exists today. However, what is done is done, and there will be no return to the pre-war days and those immediately after, when the same dogs were high in the awards in both the show ring and in field trials. Then, of course, there were only three to four hundred people involved in the breed, a great number of whom used their dogs as gundogs. Now there are many thousands who own Goldens, and the majority of the dogs will never be asked to participate in the work for which they were originally intended. An indication of the popularity of the breed is that in 1936 1,030 were registered with the Kennel Club. In 1997 the figure had risen to 15,214. The figures speak for themselves.

Earlier I mentioned that there could be either three or four judges at a field trial. As this book is for the beginner, I will explain how this works. There has to be a minimum of three judges. A dog may not be discarded from a stake, except for eliminating faults, until it has been seen by two judges. This means that a dog can have a major fault on its first retrieve and have no chance of getting an award, but it cannot be discarded. The handler has every right to continue and to go under a second judge. Experienced competitors, who know they have to hope, seldom carry on, they withdraw. However, a novice will quite often go on. I have had such things said to me, when judging, as, 'Oh, my dog needs the retrieves.' The answer to this is that if the dog is so short of work, he should not be participating in a field trial, which is not the place to do your training. These days, to comply with Kennel Club regulations, many societies appoint four judges, who work in pairs. Then a dog, as soon as it comes into the line, is under the jurisdiction of two judges and, should it be unfortunate enough to have a major fault early in the trial, it can be discarded. This saves time and, much more important, game.

All Field Trials are licensed by the Kennel Club – at least, all recognised ones are and, these days, there are virtually none that do not come within this category. There are two panels of judges approved by the Kennel Club. For panel 'B' a person must have judged at least four stakes under Kennel Club rules. For promotion to the 'A' list a satisfactory assessment of his/her ability must have been received from all 'A' co-judges. To get this promotion to the 'A' panel a judge, since being included on the 'B' list, must have officiated at least twice at Open and All-Aged Qualifying Stakes and at least two more stakes where 'A' panel judges have been officiating. Further, the stakes must have been run by two or more different societies registered with the Kennel Club. Regulations require that all the judges for the Retriever Championship are on the 'A' panel. At Open and All-Aged Stakes at least two judges must be on the 'A' panel and at all other stakes there must be at least one 'A' judge.

There are several routes to the status of Field Trial Champion. The winner of the Retriever Championship automatically becomes a Champion. The winner of two twenty-four dog stakes, or of one twenty-four and one twelve-dog stake becomes a Champion, as does the winner of three twelve-dog stakes. There must be a minimum of sixteen dogs actually running in a twenty-four dog stake and eight in a twelve-dog stake for it to count towards the title of Champion. (Some changes have been made, contact the Kennel Club for an update.) All the stakes must be Qualifying ones and, in each combination, one of the stakes must be open to all varieties of retrievers. Becoming a Champion is no mean task!

For every Golden running in trials today, there must be at least six Labradors. Not very long ago there were probably twelve Labradors to one retriever. However, a good Golden will hold his own in any company. His style of working is different from that of a Labrador. Instinctively, a Golden will cover more ground, if allowed, and normally he takes a line, that is picks up a scent, with his head carried higher than that of a retriever of another breed. This often leads to inexperienced judges believing that a Golden is running spare, a term used when a dog is galloping around doing nothing, when in actual fact it is taking a line at speed. I have, over the years, on several occasions known a co-judge come to that conclusion and within seconds the falsely accused dog has picked a strong runner!

Some thirty to forty years ago, there was a very obvious prejudice by many field trial judges against Goldens. Fortunately, this is something one seldom comes across these days, but, alas, it did happen and it made the task of those trialling Goldens that much harder. Since the last war there have been three Goldens who have won the Retriever Championship. In 1952 it was won by Jean Train's Field Trial Champion Treunair Cala (Jean Train is now Mrs Lumsden). I had a particular interest in this as Mrs Charlesworth mated her Dual Champion Noranby Destiny to Cala and I had booked a dog and a bitch puppy out of the litter. Alas, Destiny was getting on in years; she produced only two puppies and one, if not both, was born dead. The next occasion when the championship was won by a Golden was in 1954, when June Atkinson took the title with Field Trial Champion Mazurka of Wynford. It was not until 1982 that the Blue Ribbon again came to Goldens, when Robert Atkinson, June's son, won with Field Trial Champion Little Marston Chorus of Holway. In the intervening years it was a case of so near and yet so far: Eric Baldwin was second in 1966 with Field Trial Champion Palgrave Teal of Westley and again in 1978 with Field Trial Champion Volvo of Palgrave. Between those two events, in 1975, Roy Taylor, that great trial supporter from Scotland, was again close to making it a Golden year when he was third with Field Trial Champion Palgrave Zilla of Ardyle.

When one talks of Goldens and field trialling, two names immediately come to mind: those of June Atkinson and Eric Baldwin. The former has made up over twenty Field Trial Champions, whilst the latter has ten to his credit, five Goldens and five Labradors. There are other great names too numerous to list and many of these date back to the dual-purpose era. There was Bill Hickmott, who made up Stubblesdown Golden Lass to a Dual Champion in 1949. In 1950 Mrs Charlesworth made Noranby Destiny, whom I have already mentioned, a Dual Champion. Not many years later, Miss Lucy Ross's David of Westley, bred by Joan Gill who had many good dual-purpose dogs, gained his title as an International Dual Champion. He was the only dog within the breed to achieve this distinction and, undoubtedly, the last one to do so, for the rift between work and show has become too great to bridge. David was handled throughout his working career by Jim Cranston, one of the greats in the annals of all-round gundog trainers. It was a combination I particularly remember, for the very good reason that I played second fiddle to them on more than one occasion. In the first Open Stake that David won, I owned and handled the second and third! There were so many dual-purpose kennels throughout the 1950s and 1960s that it would be impossible to name them all. It would, however, be fair to say that the majority of kennels of note both showed and worked their dogs, supplying an excellent supporting cast at the Trials, and allowing the stars to shine!

To return to the education of you and your puppy, who by now will be an adult, the greatest schoolmaster you can have from now on is experience. Theory won't win trials; it provides a base to work from, but you've got to get out and take part in the real thing. Picking up is fine and it gives experience to your dog but, normally, you haven't time to try spectacular retrieves. If you can become friendly with one or two top handlers, try to join them for training sessions. You will accomplish far more from that than from the general mêlée of picking up. There will be less to distract your lad and you will be able really to test his ability. Further, if you keep your eyes and ears open, you'll learn a lot from your companions.

I was never a totally dedicated field trialler; my interest in Goldens has always been universal but first and foremost I regard them as working gundogs. At one stage of my life I was fortunate enough to be able to shoot two days a week and frequently three. Nevertheless, I have had a modest share of success in trialling dual-purpose dogs and would like to proffer a little advice to beginners. When you enter your first trial, remember that you are doing it for pleasure, so don't become tense. If you do this, the tension will go down the lead to your dog and, suddenly, your biddable boy will be as worked up as you when sent for a bird and, as a result, will not react as he should to your instructions. Never panic if you think your dog is going wrong and don't start blowing on your whistle as if it were the pipes of Pan. As is said today, keep your cool. Sometimes, not often, you can get away with murder!

I remember one case when I was shooting at a two-day stake. We were in sugar-beet and I winged a cock pheasant, which was off at a rate of knots. A dog was sent immediately, it was a real potterer and, rightly, was called up almost at once. A second dog was sent; its handler was working from almost directly in front of where I stood with the head gamekeeper. Immediately in line with us was a place where the seed drill had become blocked and there was a strip of bare ground about 50 yds long and 1 yd wide, stretching away over the brow of the hill. The judge a few yards to the right could not see this. The dog reached the fall and was working with great style. The next thing that happened was that a rabbit appeared, running straight down the clear area. It was hotly pursued by the dog and away they went out of sight. Lesser handlers would have panicked, there would have been piercing blasts on the whistle, yells of 'No' and the game would have been given away. This handler glanced at the judge, who could see the back of the dog but not the rabbit, and kept his hands in his pockets! After several minutes the dog returned with the pheasant, which he had obviously run into by chance. The keeper whispered to me, 'Fur seems to have changed to feathers.' The handler grinned and, equally quietly, said, 'Yes, he's lost a couple of legs too.' We all need a bit of luck at times; he went on and won the stake!

Never refuse to put your dog on the lead if you are given the opportunity. Often, when you are in a root crop and have come to the end of a strip, the judge will tell you that you *may* put your dog on the lead whilst the line is getting sorted out ready for the next walk. Technically, you are still under the judge's orders. Twice I have seen such an offer ignored with dire consequences. Once I put a dog out for chasing a rabbit as we were walking along a headland. Another time a co-judge discarded a dog that dived into the hedge and pegged a pheasant, that is, picked a bird that had not been shot or sent for. Always accept the judge's decision; he sees more of the work than you do. You may not agree, but you may not as yet know enough to appreciate all the fine points of judging and you are not the judge. Field trialling has no room for bad losers.

One final point. Many beginners become very worked up if asked to send their dog for a woodcock or snipe. I've often had it said to me when judging a Puppy/Novice, 'Oh, I don't think he'll pick that, he's never had one.' The answer is to make sure he will. Years ago, when I lived in Ireland and did a lot of snipe shooting, I used to train my puppies on starlings. Once a puppy had picked a few of them, I never had him refuse to pick either a snipe or woodcock.

The Qualifier

Dedicated to
Kelly – Champion Stolford Happy Lad

Frolicking, rollicking, gaysome o' Stern,
Kelly, my lad, there's a lot you've to learn.
Lots you've to learn about work and its needs,
So come on, old son, try a dummy from reeds.

Pouncing and bouncing and wild as a hawk,
'Heel up, old boy, you're not just out to walk!'
Forget the Show Champion and things that you're not,
Settle down, use your brains, you must learn about shot.

Learn about scent and hunting and beet,
Retrieving to hand – make it quick, clean and neat.
Six seasons you've spent – not a feel of a bird,
For a Golden of quality that's just absurd.

A few weeks from now I shall know if you've tried,
Before judges you'll be – to get Qualified.
So it's 'Get out there, hi lost', your nose to the ground,
Sitting, retrieving and making no sound.

Time passed so quickly; you've learned a great deal.
Tomorrow that blot on your escutcheon we'll heal.
We'll delete the word 'Show', of that I've no doubt,
For you've learned to love shooting and what it's about.

Now we're in line, under quizzical stare;
Off the lead for a shot – Kelly, move if you dare!
There's a partridge, another, two dead on the grass,
Just get one, old fellow, and you're sure of a pass.

One's back to hand, all slobber but sound.
Passed now to the judge – you're through I'll be bound!
What's this – back to the line – not quite enough cover,
Kelly, you must hunt for the game you recover!

THE QUALIFIER

So into the beet with judges we go,
One going forward – a partridge to throw.
'Send your dog now' but he's gone with a bang.
He's a boy for this hunting, he soon got the hang.

The bird is to hand – the judges are pleased;
For handler and friends the tension is eased.
Kelly, you are a gundog, a Champion at last,
That bend-sinister title's removed from your past.

Frolicking, rollicking, fearless and gay,
Kelly, old son, I wish you could stay;
But it's back to your life full of leisure and fun,
Between you and me we've both lost a great chum.

Michael F. Twist

Ch Stolford Happy Lad (Sire Stolford Playboy, dam Prystina of Wymondham). BOB Crufts 1976. 19 CCs. The only dog in the breed to have sired BOB at Crufts for three consecutive years. 1979 Ch Brensham Audacity, 1980. Sh Ch Cattrysse Chevalier, 1981 Ch Bryanstown Gaucho. Owner Mrs Peggy Robertson, Breeder Mr P. Ranger

13

Show Gundog Working Certificate

The Show Gundog Working Certificate, for many years known as a Qualifying Certificate, is exactly what it says, a certificate saying that a show dog still retains its basic natural instinct to work. This certificate, which I shall refer to as the SGWC is required to enable an owner to claim the title of Champion, as opposed to Show Champion, having won three Challenge Certificates in the show ring. An award in any field trial also fulfils the necessary Kennel Club requirements. However, unfortunately only a few dogs attain their title via this road, which is sad but, alas, a sign of the times.

The work requirements as laid down by the Kennel Club are both minimal and simple. There are three main essentials: that a dog has shown that it is not gun-shy and was off the lead during gunfire; that it will hunt; and that it will retrieve tenderly. The regulations go on to say that steadiness is not essential, but that whining and barking are eliminating faults. Meeting these requirements is not very difficult if a dog has not had work bred out of it, but if you are attempting to do that it does require a little time and preparation.

The Kennel Club regulations governing a SGWC are adequate if, in some cases, totally illogical. It would be my guess that the reason for this is that the regulations are drawn up by the Field Trial Committee, who have little or no interest in the show side of dogs and have not really thought their regulations through on this matter.

You can go about obtaining a SGWC in two ways. First, if your dog has won a Challenge Certificate at a Championship Show, then you can enter him for his certificate at a Field Trial, providing the organising society are prepared to accept this. They are under no obligation to do so. One of the judges must be on the 'A' panel. Now comes the bit which to me seems totally irrational. I quote from the regulations, 'The Society holding the Meeting is recognised for the Retriever Championship Stake.' What possible bearing can the status of the society have on awarding a SGWC? The activities of the society are irrelevant: it is the judges who award the SGWC, not the society. The result of the ruling is that an 'A' judge acting for a society that runs a Qualifying Stake for the Championship can, with his co-judges, award a SGWC. The following week the same team of judges, officiating for a society that does not run a Qualifying Stake for the Championship, would be unable to award an SGWC!

As I have said, there is another way of going after your SGWC, as laid down in Kennel Club Regulation 21. This reads as follows:

A gundog which has won one or more first prizes in a Class for its breed at a Show where Challenge Certificates are offered for the breed, may be entered for a Show Gundog Working Certificate at a Specialist Club Show Gundog Working Trial provided that Judge or Judges of the Trial are on Panel 'A' for the breed.

That is much the best way of gaining the SGWC for, to use the old terminology, qualifiers are seldom really welcome at a trial. The regulations say that they must be seen before lunch. The judges get through a round in the trial and are about to break for lunch, when up comes the secretary to say that there are two or three qualifiers to be seen. This usually ends up with a gun staying back to fire shots and with birds being thrown into cover. Everything is rushed and I have, on several occasions, heard the owners complaining of the scant attention they have been given. I am sure that from the owner's point of view a Show Gundog Working Trial is better. There is another anomaly here. A specialist club, entitled to run a Show Gundog Working Trial but not recognised to run a stake qualifying for the Retriever Championship, could run such a trial. The same club could then run a Field Trial, inviting the judges who officiated at the Show Gundog Working Trial, but would not be permitted to accept the entry of a dog that had won a Challenge Certificate and whose owner wished to try for its SGWC. To me this doesn't make sense, but then nor have other things that the Kennel Club have done in this connection in the past.

For those who have not been to a Show Gundog Working Trial, this is what normally happens. I say 'normally', because there have been cases where the judges have tried to run the event like a field trial, which is not what is required, by asking dogs to jump fences, swim rivers and try for birds that have been down for half an hour or more. Such activities are not part of the Kennel Club requirements. The way the likes of Eric Baldwin, Frank Clitheroe – another of the greats and the only person to win first and second in the Retriever Championship in the same year – Joan Gill and, indeed, myself would conduct the trial is as follows. You would be taken into the line, that is the line of guns who are spaced out thirty-five to forty yards apart. Each of the two judges would take a number of dogs. All dogs would be on the lead. Each judge would space his dogs out between two guns, the lowest number on the right. The judge whom you were under would explain that when a bird looked as though it was coming over one of the guns close to you, he would tell you to take the lead off your dog. If the bird was shot and your dog ran in and picked it, that would not matter. However, should he high-tail it into the distance through fright, then you would have failed. If he sat, so much the better; you would be told to put him back on the lead. That part of the test would be over.

Next you would be asked to retrieve a bird from cover. It might be from a woodland, a root crop or long rough grass. The main thing in that situation is that there is sufficient cover to make him work. Therefore, you would want to be able to send your dog out to hunt. This is important as you may not always get a mark. If your dog hunts, finds a bird and retrieves it tenderly to hand, that's fine and your troubles are over. However, if he does not find a bird, but has worked the ground well, don't panic; you'll be given a chance of a retrieve later providing he has made a genuine and sustained effort at hunting. If this happens you are two-thirds of the way to getting what you are after. For a retrieve you may be asked to send for a bird lying out in an open field, or the judge may throw one. All your dog has to do is to retrieve it tenderly. This should be no problem IF you have taken the trouble and a little time to prepare your dog for what you want him to do. Once you have achieved this, you have fulfilled the third requirement and, in due course, you will receive your SGWC.

I have already covered all aspects of the limited amount of training that is necessary to obtain a SGWC, even including the best way of going about obtaining game to train your dog. However, I have known people bring their dog to a Show Gundog Working Trial never having seen a pheasant or, for that matter, even a pigeon! It is greatly to the credit of some of the dogs that they have gone out and retrieved a bird without any great problem. I remember a dog who was brought to a Trial being sent for a pheasant; never having seen one, he registered his opinion by cocking his leg on it! Kennel Club regulations say, 'A dog may not run for a Show Gundog Working Certificate more than three times in all and not more that twice in any one Field Trial season.' The owner on this occasion borrowed a pheasant and, when the judges had gone through the card, asked if his dog could be seen again. They agreed. The dog hunted and retrieved a pheasant in good style – this time he knew what he was supposed to do! That afternoon the owner of the shoot invited any who wished to stay and pick up. The Trial had finished at lunch-time. The competitor whose dog had shown such disdain for the pheasant in the morning was one of those to stay. His dog did several useful retrieves, including getting a duck from the river. By dark both dog and handler were bitten by the work bug. Although the dog was no longer a puppy, the owner set about training him and he did that well, which was made all the more meritorious by the fact that he lived in London. The leg-cocking dog went on to become a very useful trial dog, winning a number of awards, including some in Any-Variety Qualifying Stakes. It all proves that where there's a will there's a way.

Another to prove the same point was the late Eddie Orton, whose Mossbridge Challenger became the first English and Irish Champion. The Irish Kennel Club, in their wisdom, did not allow Show Champions nor, for that matter, could a dog obtain its title as Field Trial Champion without qualifying on the bench! When Eddie had won the required number of Green Star points, he had to get his working certificate in Ireland before he could claim the title of Irish Champion for Challenger. Eddie lived in the middle of an industrial city in Lancashire. He told me that he knew nothing about training, so he bought a book on the subject. Then he found, or maybe he arranged, a loose upright in the paling round one of the local public parks, which was normally locked until around 9.00 a.m. He bought pigeons from a poulterer and, several mornings a week, made his way stealthily at dawn into the park to train his dog. He knew that in Ireland, as well as having to do what is required here, his dog would have to retrieve from water. The park lake, therefore came in for regular use as well as the flower-beds, which he used for cover! Eddie crossed on the night boat from Liverpool, and took a train to within seventeen miles of the shoot where the Field Trial was being held in the west of Ireland and a taxi for the remainder of the way. Challenger did one of the hardest and best qualifiers I have ever seen. My wife and I took both the very happy owner and his dog to the boat in Dublin that evening. He was home around 8.00 a.m. the following morning, and that really demonstrates what I call enthusiasm!

Finally, on this subject, the title of Champion is well worth striving for; it is worth the effort to obtain it and it makes life much more fun for your dog!

14

Showing

Having gone through the various stages from puppyhood to field trial level to develop your boy's working instincts, we now come to the reverse side of the coin – showing. This is an aspect of dogs that greatly appeals to me and is the reason why, for some fifty years, my interest has been in dual-purpose Goldens. I do like symmetry and balance in all animals and have, in years gone by, also been extensively involved in showing horses, ponies, several breeds of cattle, sheep and pigs.

To prepare and train your puppy for show is far less exacting and time consuming than teaching him to work. Nevertheless, to be successful, you will require similar dedication and determination to reach the top, particularly now that entries are so large and the competition great. Showing is a road fraught with disappointment, frustration and exasperation, as well as being enlivened with moments of great exultation. You have to accept that beauty is in the eye of the beholder; if you cannot do this, then keep out of showing. There will be times when you are certain that yours is the best dog and yet the judge will throw you out with the rough. In the 1945–6 Golden Retriever Club's *Victory Year Book* King George V's Maxims appear. The following lines are taken from these:

> Teach me to be obedient to the rules of the game.
> Teach me to win if I may; if I may not win, then above all, teach me to be a good loser.

Dwell on these words before entering the world of showing. If you do, make them your maxims and, at all times, abide by them.

Before dealing with the preparations of your puppy for the show ring, it would be as well to list the various types of shows run under the rules and regulations of the Kennel Club. They are:

1. Exemption Shows.
2. Sanction Shows.
3. Limited Shows.
4. Open Shows.
5. Championship Shows, where KC Challenge Certificates are on offer.

Ch Stanroph Sailor Boy, 9CCs 5 BOB and 10 Res CCs bred and owned by Mrs Anne Woodcock, leading breeder for 1994/95/96/97 and won the most CCs (9) in 1997.

There can be up to 16 classes in each sex, plus Brace and Special classes a Full classification for all sections can be obtained from the Kennel Club.

Whilst Champions may be exhibited at Open Shows, there is a tradition in Goldens which has led to this being considered unsporting and it is definitely not the done thing. Some would argue that by not exhibiting the top dogs within the breed, such honours as Best in Show are left open to those in other breeds who have no such scruples. In spite of this, Goldens seem to acquire their share of this major award. A similar practice is applied to showing a dog under a judge who has given it a Challenge Certificate. Again there is no rule either of the Kennel Club or breed clubs that forbids this. The exceptions are Crufts and The Golden Retriever Club Show; now there are fourteen breed clubs! Again this is something which is by no means the accepted rule for many other breeds. Admittedly only one Challenge Certificate from an individual judge counts towards the title of Champion and I have heard it argued that by showing again under the same judge one is possibly depriving another exhibitor of a Challenge Certificate which is badly needed towards a title. This is not really a logical

Ch Camrose Cabus Christopher (Sire Ch Camrose Tallyrand of Anbria, dam Cabus Baltby Charmer). Winner of 41 CCs, sire of 33 CC winners of which 26 were champions. Owner Mrs J. Tudor. Breeder Mrs Z. Moriarty.

argument as one could say the same about every Challenge Certificate a dog wins after obtaining the three required for its title! However, basically I think it is a sound custom, although personally I would like to see classes for Champions and, once they are made up, to see dogs becoming ineligible to compete for Challenge Certificates. That happens in a number of countries.

For those who do not know exactly how a Challenge Certificate is obtained, the procedure is as follows. In all breeds that are numerically strong, like Goldens, the Kennel Club offer two Challenge Certificates. Normally there are two judges, one for each sex. When a judge has completed his/her classes, all unbeaten dogs or bitches from Minor Puppy through to Open and, where there is one, the Field Trial class, are brought into the ring. They compete against each other for their respective Challenge Certificates. The winning dog and bitch then meet for the judges to decide the Best of Breed. The outright winner goes on to contest the Gundog Group, made up of all the Best of Breeds from the gundog section. Finally, the winners of the seven groups come together for the Best in Show to be decided.

Ch Styal Stefanie of Camrose (Sire Ch Camrose Cabus Christopher, dam Ch Styal Sibella). Top winning bitch of all times, 27 CCs. Owners Mrs J. Tudor and Miss R. Wilcock. Breeder Mrs H. Hinks.

As I said in an earlier chapter, a Champion or Show Champion is a dog or bitch which has won three Challenge Certificates under three different judges. To acquire the former title, a SGWC or a Field Trial award is required. There is, in addition, a junior title, namely a Junior Warrant. This is issued by the Kennel Club on application by the owner of a dog that has obtained twenty-five points at shows whilst under the age of 18 months. First prizes in breed classes at Championship Shows, where Challenge Certificates are offered, count as three points each. One point is given for each first prize won in breed classes at Open Shows. First prizes in other classes, other than breed classes, do not count.

If you have a desire to exhibit your puppy, then, before doing so, attend a few shows to see what is required with regard to presentation and conformation. To acquire an eye for the latter will take both time and experience. There are those who are unable to acquire an eye and, for however long they are showing, all their geese will remain swans! Do not take your boy with you so that he can have a look too! Kennel Club Regulations (NB: The KC are constantly changing both numbers and regulations) says that no animal other than an exhibit shall be brought into the precincts of a dog show.

To make things more difficult for the beginner, these days there are different types within the breed. All you can do is select the one that has the most appeal for you and stick with it. A dog may win a Challenge Certificate; at the next show, under a different judge, it may get nothing! I mentioned having been involved in showing a variety of livestock; in none have I met the inconsistency in judging that one finds with dogs. Having said this, there is only one breed standard. The inconsistency comes from the individual interpretations of the standard and from the judges' personal likes and dislikes.

The completely faultless dog, and indeed completely faultless animal of any kind, still has to be bred, for even in the very best there is some room for improvement. That is one of the fascinating aspects of breeding any livestock – there is a desire to achieve

Ch Nortonwood Fanus
(Sire Ch Camrose Cabus Christopher, dam Nortonwood Fantasy of Milo). Winner of 13 CCs. Leading gundog sire 1984, 1985. Top progeny sire all breeds 1986. Owners/Breeders Mr & Mrs F. R. Bradbury.

perfection! In an earlier chapter I gave a short résumé of what to look for when selecting a puppy. However, before embarking on showing your lad, a more in-depth look at correct conformation should be made. What makes up that ideal picture of a top show Golden? Symmetry and balance are essential, giving a sense of the strength and stamina essential for a day's work in the shooting field. An alert and kindly expression is a must. The head should be free from coarseness or skin wrinkles. It should be broad across the skull, being neither flat nor domed. The length of the foreface, that is from the nose to the stop, should be approximately equal to that from the stop to the occiput. The former should be well-defined, but not to the extent of the dog being dish-faced, that is, concave. The eyes should be dark and set well apart. They should be neither small nor slanting and they should be dark around the rims. The ears, situated virtually level with the eyes, should be of moderate size. The jaws should be strong with a good scissor bite, as already mentioned. The muzzle should be deep and wide, but not to the extent of coarseness. A snipey, that is a narrow, pointed muzzle, is undesirable. The nose should preferably be black and the whole head should have a balanced and well-chiselled appearance, being well set on the neck.

The neck should be of such a length that it looks neither elongated nor stuffy. It should be clean and muscular, with no throatiness or dewlap, leading to well-laid-back shoulders. To achieve this, the shoulder-blade (the scapula) and the upper arm (the humerus) should be at an angle of approximately 90° to each other. This will give a slope of around 45° from the point of the shoulder to the withers and ensures that the forelegs are correctly placed under the body. The greater the angle between the shoulder-blade and the upper arm, the straighter the shoulder. The reach of neck and the slope of the shoulder are interrelated, as any who are involved with horses will know. Get up on a straight-shouldered horse and there is nothing in front of you – and you are left with a great loop of spare reins! On a well-fronted horse there is plenty of neck in front of you and, when cantering in the show ring, you have little in the way of surplus reins. With a straight-shouldered horse one gets a short, choppy or hackney action, giving an uncomfortable ride. The same applies to dogs. Bad conformation means bad movement. Often when judging, as dogs are going around the ring I mentally throw a saddle on them. Alas, these days, there are far too many with which, if they were horses, one would have too much rein and an uncomfortable ride, for they have a prancing hackney action brought about by wrong angulation of the shoulder.

The withers, the apex of the shoulder-blades, should be of moderate width. It is hard to be specific about an exact measurement, but, from a number of random checks done on dogs with good shoulders, it would seem that three and a half inches to four and a half inches is about average. With my thumb and little finger fully extended I can span nine inches. Some years ago, judging on the Continent, I came across a Champion whom I was unable to span across the withers in this way! Excessive width is frequently found with straight shoulders, giving an unbalanced and heavy appearance to a dog's front. Conversely, if the shoulder-blades are too close together, the dog will be narrow in front and the width between the legs will be narrow also. The forelegs should be straight if viewed from the front or side, with good bone; this means neither too fine, giving a spindly look, nor too heavy, giving a coarse and heavy appearance. Pasterns should be nearly straight, with just enough angulation for them to act as effective shock-absorbers, thus ensuring that the weight is evenly distributed over all pads. Unfortunately, this is something quite frequently ignored by many judges today. If a dog is down on its pasterns, then the weight is incorrectly distributed and it cannot move as it should. If you look at the foreleg of a foxhound, you will see that they are, virtually dead straight, to the extent of almost knuckling over; these dogs are bred to gallop for hours. Don't forget that a Golden is a gundog and should be able to do the same thing! Fortunately, if a dog is down on its pasterns, this can often be rectified or certainly improved by plenty of steady road work. The feet should be round, like those of a cat, and of medium size. Open, splayed or pointed feet are a fault.

The body should be well coupled and balanced. The top line, from the neck to the croup, should be level and not dropping away at the tail. If you are wondering what 'well coupled' means, it is that the space between the end of the rib-cage and the pelvis, the loin, should be of medium length. You do not want the appearance of an over-long body; nor should it be so short as to appear cobby. The whole should be balanced and deep through the heart. The ribs should be well sprung, in other words, correctly rounded or arched: not excessively, so the dog is barrel shaped, nor too straight, so he is flat sided. The latter can be deceptive when taking a lateral view of a dog and it is only when one goes over it that the fault becomes apparent. The rib structure must be such that it allows the maximum expansion of the lungs when required. Lack of depth through the heart gives a 'shelly' and rather weedy look. The tail should be set on so that it gives the appearance of a

Ch Styal Scott of Glendilde (Sire Ch Nortonswood Fanus, dam Ch Styal Susila). Top winning dog of all times, 42 CCs. Owners Mr and Mrs R. Sckoles. Breeder Mrs H. Hinks.

continuing straight line from the back and it should be carried level with this when the dog is moving. It should not curl, even at the tip, and it should be of such a length as to reach the hock. It is quite common to see a dog carrying its tail almost vertically; this is known as flying the flag and it definitely detracts from the overall picture when a dog is going round the ring.

Now we move on to the power-house, the hindquarters. This is where all the drive and get up and go comes from. Both the loin and the legs must be strong and muscular and good second thighs are essential but, alas, frequently lacking these days! When a dog is comfortable and standing four-square, the hocks, viewed from the rear, should be straight. If they turn in, the dog is what is known as cow-hocked. Viewed from the side, the line from the hocks to the feet should be straight. The angulation in the hindquarters should be basically the same as in the forequarters, the tibia being at an angle of 90° from the femur. This joint is normally referred to as the stifle. The correct angulation gives what is known as a good turn of stifle; lack of it produces a straight stifle and excess results in sickle-hocks (that is to say, when a dog is standing naturally, instead of the feet being directly below the hocks they are forward, making the lower leg curved). Both cow-hocks and sickle-hocks are major faults. When a dog is placed correctly in the show ring, the rear feet should be further apart than the front. When standing comfortably and to the best advantage, the hind feet will be slightly behind a line straight down from the hips. Both the thighs and second thighs should be well muscled down to the hocks.

Now we come to the all-important question of movement, which is largely, but not entirely, governed by construction. A dog with poor conformation cannot be a really good mover. On the other hand, one correctly put together which has been overfed and lacks proper exercise can be a poor mover. What you are looking for is a dog which, when viewed from the front or the rear, moves its legs in straight lines, with elbows tight in at the sides. The legs should not turn in or out, and the feet should not cross or touch. However, the faster a dog moves, the more the feet will come closer together, towards the central line of gravity. When a dog is moved, in the show ring, it is trotting. Viewed from the side it should appear to flow over the ground with a long, effortless and even stride. With this gait the legs diagonally opposite to each other move back and forth simultaneously, the front foot leaving the ground fractionally ahead of the oncoming back one. There should be an obvious thrust from the hind legs, but without undue exertion being apparent. As I have said, the movement should appear effortless, with no sign of rolling when viewed from the rear. The front movement should be free of any prancing or hackney action. That would produce a short choppy stride, lacking extension. To use a horsy term, the effect would be of galloping on the same bit of ground.

Finally, the coat may be flat or wavy, with good feathering and a dense water-resisting undercoat. The colour may be any shade of gold or cream. In height dogs should be 22 to 24 in at the shoulder (56 to 61 cm); bitches should be 20 to 22 in (51 to 56 cm).

If you intend to show your lad right from the start, then you can begin training from an early age. When you've finished grooming, stand him four-square, putting a hand under his jaw to keep his head up and straight, also hold his tail out in line with his back or fractionally below it. Do not hold his head and tail up in an exaggerated and unnatural position, in what I call the banana stance; it is unsightly and does not do credit to any dog! Whilst on the subject of stances, there are handlers who extend both forelegs and hindlegs, so that the poor dog is overstretched and uncomfortable and looks as though it is trying to emulate a hackney horse! Others try the reverse and push their dog's legs in under

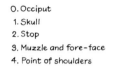

0. Occiput
1. Skull
2. Stop
3. Muzzle and fore-face
4. Point of shoulders

5. Chest
6. Brisket
7. Pastern
8. Ribs
9. Withers

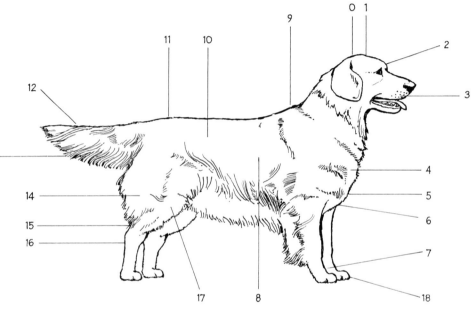

10. Loin
11. Croup
12. Tail
13. Feathering

14. Thighs
15. Second thighs
16. Hocks
17. Stifles
18. Feet round and cat like.

A. Correct stance – standing foursquare, comfortable, showing to advantage on loose lead.

B. Over-stretched – uncomfortable, legs incorrectly placed, depicting a poor image.

C. Concertinaed – a common fault with many over-anxious handlers!

D. Topped and tailed – legs correctly placed, comfortable, showing level top line, good reach of neck and turn of stifle.

E. The banana stance – over-stretched, uncomfortable, head and tail too high.

F. Front view – legs correctly spaced and comfortable.

G. *'Anyone for croquet?' – forelegs much too far apart. This position usually achieved by lifting with hand between forelegs when placing.*

H. *'What's this all about?' – uncertainty due to lack of training. Illustrates straight stifle and lack of second thigh, compare with the correctness of A.*

them so that the dog assumes an unnatural position. Avoid these excesses from the start. Remember that a little and often applies to any training, so, with the very young, make each lesson a matter of seconds rather than of minutes. If you overdo it, you will find you have an obedient, but totally bored and uninterested puppy who is not going to show the sparkle that is all-important in the show ring.

The lead work and heeling, already dealt with, is also relevant to showing. When you come in from any such training, before finally ending the session stand your puppy up, placing his front and back legs. Do this by putting one hand under his jaw and the other over his shoulder and in under his body, just behind the elbows. Lift up his forequarters four of five inches and drop him down. His legs will normally, arrive in the correct place. Whatever you do, don't lift him with your hand between his front legs. If you do, the chances are that you will finish up with his forelegs too wide apart and looking like a croquet hoop! Then put your hand over his tail and between his hind legs, lift his hindquarters and, again, drop him down. If you have done this correctly, he should be standing pretty well four-square. You may have to make some small individual adjustment to a leg, but make sure that when you have done this he is standing with his weight evenly and correctly distributed, so that he is comfortable. All the time you are placing him, keep saying 'Stand'. When he is doing this exercise reasonably well, move in front of him, holding the sides of his head. Then take your hands away and leaving the lead loose, tell him, 'Stand'. If he tries to sit – and the chances are that at this stage of his training you will have been teaching him to do just that – put a hand under him, lift him up and give the command 'No. Stand.' He will quickly get the idea and know what is wanted. It will not be long before, when you move in front of him and tell him to stand, he will be standing four-square. You may have to make slight adjustments but, basically, he will put himself in the correct position because it is the most comfortable. Talk to him and give him tidbits, but only when he's standing still. Encourage him to wag his tail and show animation, this will always catch the judge's eye in the showing.

As I have already made quite clear, I am a great believer in doing initial training in private, this applies to training for the ring as much as it does to training for the field. In addition to standing, you must teach your puppy to run out on a loose lead, gaiting as has already been described. As well as going in a straight line, practise running in a triangle. You will frequently be asked to do this in the show ring so that the judge can observe rear, lateral and front movement. It is most important that your puppy is not pulling away from you; if that happens he will be leaning, his legs will be not moving in straight lines and it will be impossible for a judge to assess his movement.

When your puppy has turned 4½ months start taking him to training classes. I have particularly specified this age for a very good reason, which is that he should have had the extra parvo innoculation which I mentioned earlier at 4 months. He will, therefore, have the maximum immunisation that you can give him against parvo virus. You should have no great trouble in finding a training class near you. If you do, make enquiries of your local veterinary surgeons and if they cannot help you contact the Kennel Club. A large number of general all-breed canine societies run classes. There are around six hundred of these registered with the Kennel Club and another five hundred specialising in training. You want to be clear about what you require, namely training in ring craft, not obedience. When you have enrolled with a club, take your lad along once a week. It will give an excellent opportunity to get him used to being in the company of other dogs. The person taking the class will go over him as a judge would in the show ring, and he will become used to being handled by strangers. It will also give him confidence in readiness for being in the close proximity of a number of people and dogs. Once he has ceased to worry about people and a lot of other dogs, if indeed he ever did, has learned to stand correctly and will run out as required, there is little point in carrying on with the classes. The chances are that if you do he'll get bored and start losing that sparkle and exuberance which can make the difference between gaining top honours and being an also-ran in the show ring.

When your pup is humanised and everybody's friend, ask someone to run him for you so that you can see his movement. As a puppy he will, most likely, be gangly, but as he matures his movement will tighten up, providing he receives plenty of road work. Even if he seems perfect, from time to time take a look. You could have him slightly overweight, causing him to roll as he moves, or there could be some other failing developing that needs to be rectified. I have often had owners whose dogs I have not placed come to me after judging to enquire what is was about their dog that I did not like. If the answer has been movement, frequently the reply to that is, 'Oh, I can't see that.' Make sure you do! Whilst both you and your puppy are learning, it is often very helpful to stand him up in front of a mirror; then you can see how you are presenting him and what mistakes, if any, you are making.

When exhibiting your dog, never drop the end of the lead. You will see this being done, but don't copy it. I have on many occasions seen a dog stood up, and the handler then drops the lead, moves to the back and holds out the tail. The dog has stood like a statue, inanimate and bored, and meanwhile the handler has been breaking Kennel Club Regulations. Should the matter be reported, the handler could be liable for disciplinary action. Further, remember that you may not receive assistance from a person outside the ring who attracts your dog's attention by any method (see Regulations). This practice is commonly referred to as double handling and it is very much frowned upon, rightly so, by the Kennel Club. It could lead to the offender being debarred from showing.

Before taking your puppy into the ring, thought must be given to presenting him to the best possible advantage. He must be well fleshed, not too fat, but carrying sufficient weight so that he does not go in over the loin. There is a tendency in many exhibitors to produce their dogs in too fat a condition. This failing is not limited to dogs; the same thing happens with horses and cattle, and indeed, almost all classes of livestock. In the case of gundogs and hunters, these are regularly produced in the show ring with such surplus of fat that a day's work would be totally out of the question! If you want to be successful, you will have to go along with the fashion. Nevertheless, man's and, indeed, woman's, desires to overfeed an animal to exhibit it is something of a contradiction. Can you imagine the contestants for Miss World all appearing like the Roly Poly's? Enough of such levity; back to your puppy. If you are going to exhibit him in Minor Puppy Classes, that is, from 6 to 9 months of age, don't overfeed him; experienced judges will make allowances for age. I have noticed that very few puppies produced at 8 or 9 months that look really mature and often swamp their opponents achieve much in later years. There are, of course, exceptions, but they are certainly not the rule. To be successful, you will have to have your boy in show condition, and you can at least make sure that any extra flesh he is carrying is firm and not just flab. This you can achieve by plenty of road work, but keep in mind what I have already said about too much exercise at an early age.

Do not waste either your time or money exhibiting your dog if he is out of coat or in the middle of casting it. Whilst this is a natural phenomenon, the competition is such today that unless your lad is in full coat you are most unlikely to win. It can happen that you will, but if so all the rest of the class will have some glaring fault! When he is in coat, then he will require trimming. It is advisable to start this about a month before you want to show him. If you intend showing on a regular basis, trimming is an on-going requirement. Once again, it is a case of a little and often. If you keep to this, then the hair will lie more naturally and scissor marks will not be obvious. Unfortunately, these days little notice seems to be taken of this and one often sees a dog, particularly a very light one, cut right back to the undercoat, especially around the neck and shoulders. To achieve any degree of trimming you will require 23-toothed double-bladed thinning scissors, mid-weight 7 or 7½ in straight scissors, a stripping knife and a comb. The last of these you should already have. If you are unable to obtain your requirements locally, you can always get the equipment from Allbrookes. Personally, I do not favour excessive trimming; cutting back to the undercoat detracts from the true beauty of a Golden and, bearing in mind that it is a gundog, apart from that it is removing coat that is there for protection when the dog is working in heavy cover. Any trimming that is done should be a matter of tidying up to make the most of a dog's natural outline and, fortu-nately, this is what most exhibitors do. The main places for attention are the tail, ears, feet, hocks, chest and around the collar, or junc-tion of the neck and shoulder. To trim correctly is quite an art and, when done properly, it greatly improves a dog's chance of success in the ring.

It does not really matter where you start to trim your dog, but I like to see a tail done first. One can then assess the overall picture and decide how much wants to come off and where. The tail should be started at the tip, sufficient hair being left to reach the hock. This varies from dog to dog according to the actual length of the bone structure of the tail. The feathering should then be shaped with the thinning scissors, so that it takes on a gradual curve as shown on the diagrammatic outline, or indeed in a number of the photographs included in this book. At the longest part, the feath-ering should be around four to four and a half inches, any long, straggling hairs being snipped off with the straight scissors. The outline of the ears should be clear and any long hairs around these should be removed. The easiest way to do this is with a stripping knife, although some people use scissors; but there is a risk with the latter method of leaving scissor marks. Next we come to the trickiest bit, that is, if the end result is to look natural, namely the shoulders and neck. Trimming can be a time-consuming operation, which is one of the reasons why you should start it well before a show. Of course, a lot depends on the individual dog and the density of the coat. Using the thinning scissors, always working upwards, it is a case of cut and comb, cut and comb. The final result should look quite level and natural, with no cutting down to the undercoat – as one not infrequently sees. There is usually an abundance of hair on the chest and brisket which will require light trimming with the thinning scissors, leaving a gently curved line from the jaw to the brisket. Don't go mad, as some people do, or you will finish up with something like a crew-cut. A Golden's coat is much of its charm and beauty; cut it all away and one might as well keep a Labrador!

Any excess hair from the hock to the back of the feet should be removed, as should any from the back of the knee (carpal joint) in front. The feathering above this should be tidied to make it uniform. Finally, the feet require attention. Remember that they should be round and cat-like. The hair should be trimmed back, as near to the pad as possible, with the straight scissors. Shape the feet as much as you can and then snip out the long hairs between the toes, but be careful not to overdo this and leave gaps between the toes.

Your boy should now be the right shape, or at least as near to it as his conformation and your skill with the scissors will allow. The next step towards his preparation is a bath. Whether you use your own or have a special tin one outside is entirely up to you. I opt for the latter; it's less messy! The density and nature of your dog's coat will determine how close to the day of the show you can bath him. If it is very thick and wavy, then you want to allow at least a couple of days to let it settle; do him the day before and you will have a positive teddy bear to take into the ring. If, however, he is either smooth-coated or very curly, then the nearer to the show the better. The smooth coat produces no problems; the very curly coat produces quite a lot, which I'll deal with in a moment.

Which shampoo you use is really a matter of individual preference; there is a wide selection of good ones available. When you prepare the bath for your dog, the water should be pleasantly warm, but not too hot. Having got him in, bail plenty of water over him to make sure his coat is truly wet before you apply the shampoo. Rub this well in and work up a good lather before thoroughly rinsing – and I do mean thoroughly. Finish off with tepid water, squeezing as much out of the coat as you can before allowing him out. After he's had a good shake, towel him and get him as dry as possible. Then apply a coat gloss or, if you prefer, a conditioner; they are really much the same. I find Ring's Coat Gloss is excellent, giving a good sheen to the coat. Spray it on lightly and keep combing in the direction you want the hair to lie, at the same time drying it with a hair-dryer. This is fine with a wavy or smooth-coated dog; the problems start with a curly-coated one. A wavy coat is quite acceptable, but a really curly one, like a drake's tail feathers, is not. The bathing and initial drying is the same for the curly-coated dog. Whilst the coat is still wet, spray him with Corramist, which is a lady's hair-conditioner, and comb his hair quickly and as flat as possible. Next wrap him round tightly, from behind the ears to the croup, with a bath-towel, you may need two, and hold it or them in place with safety-pins. Having got him cocooned, it is then just a matter of leaving him in front of a radiator or fire to dry. Most of the drying will come from his own body heat, The closer you can do this to the show and the longer the towels are left on, the better. When you take them off, his coat should be well flattened with just a slight wave. Having bathed and dried your boy, there will be probably just a little touching up to do with the scissors. This done you are ready for the off, once you have all your equipment together.

These days the majority of Open Shows are unbenched. With the exception of some breed shows, where special permission has been obtained from the Kennel Club, all Championship shows must be benched. What is benching? Basically it is a timber bench, raised up off the ground on trestles and divided into compartments or stalls with metal partitions. These, according to the Kennel Club, must be of such a design as to provide comfort and security. This is where you house your dog whilst at the show. Kennel Club Regulation 18(a) says that no dog shall be absent from its bench except for the purpose of being prepared for exhibition, judged or exercised. Further, the rules state that no dog must be absent from its bench for the purpose of being exercised for more than fifteen minutes. These rules are not strictly enforced, but they most certainly must not be ignored.

You will have to spend a lot of time sitting with your dog at a Championship show. It would be most unwise to leave him without at least having someone keeping an eye on him for you. Dogs have been stolen off the bench, poisoned and generally got at. My wife and I had experience of this once, many years ago, at Crufts. We had taken a kennelmaid with us to stay with the dogs when we were not at the benching. She left them for literally only a few minutes. When she returned, she found that one of the dogs, a champion, had, according to the vets, received a vicious blow about two inches from the root of the tail; they thought it had been done with the side of a grooming brush. He was in great pain; he had to be withdrawn from exhibition and was very lucky not to lose his tail. There have been numerous incidents of dogs being scissored and great lumps of coat cut off when they have been left unattended on the bench. I hasten to add that such happenings are virtually always the work of vandals, not of fellow exhibitors.

The final job is to prepare your show bag. I will assume that you are getting ready for a Championship show. You will require a bench blanket for your dog to lie on, and a bench-chain and collar to tie him up. Don't rely on a lead, for if you do have to leave him for any reason he could chew through that and be gone by the time you return. If you cannot get a suitable collar and bench-chain locally, wait until you are at a show; normally there will be a number of trade stands which sell what you require. You will need your grooming kit, plus your scissors in case any last-minute trimming is required, and also a show lead – this should be of webbing with a metal ring in the end, that is a slip lead. Never show a dog on a collar and lead; you want to be able to slacken the lead so that the judge can see the neck. Never use a choke-chain, unless it is really necessary to enable you to control him. A bottle of water and a drinking bowl are a must. I always include Neo-Sulphentrin, just in case one of the dogs gets an upset tummy, and Sulphanilamide powder to treat any cut or bite. Twice I have had a dog bitten, I hasten to add not by a Golden, but by a dog of another breed, when waiting to go into the ring. For many years I included a little pot of butter as once, going into a show, our dogs, together with a number of others, walked in some tar. Fortunately a friend had brought a picnic lunch and was able to give me some butter to clean them up. A tin of Johnson's Baby Powder is useful if a dog is stained walking in to the show. It makes quite a good cleaning agent when applied and then brushed out. A folding chair will be most useful, whether the show is benched or unbenched. Lastly, when you've everything loaded into the car, don't forget the dog! Believe me, you would not be creating a precedent – it has been done!

Mr Jim Gale's Ft Ch Earnsfield Teal and Ft Ch Ben of Cadicote.

15

Obedience and Agility

Obedience classes have become very popular and the growth in this sector has been very marked over the past twenty years. The classes have become highly competitive and are fully controlled by the Kennel Club. There are six grades or classes; in each of these the exercises are specified by the governing body, as are the number of points available, the classes are:

1. Pre-Beginners (five exercises with a total of 75 points) for dogs and owners who have not won a first in any Obedience Competition.
2. Beginners (six exercises with a total of 100 points) open to those owners, handlers and dogs who have not won two or more firsts in Beginners' Classes, or a first in any other Obedience Class.
3. Novice (eight exercises with a total of 100 points) for dogs that have not won two firsts in Obedience Classes (Beginners' Classes excepted).
4. Class A (nine exercises with a total of 150 points) for dogs that have not won two firsts in Obedience Classes (Beginners' Classes excepted).
5. Class B (seven exercises with a maximum of 200 points) for dogs which have not won a total of three firsts in Classes B or C.
6. Class C (seven exercises with a total of 300 points) at Championship shows, for dogs which have been placed at least once not lower than third in Novice Class or A and B Classes and have won an Open Class C with no fewer than 290 marks, and have also gained 290 marks or more on three other occasions in Open Class C under three different judges.

At Championship shows two Obedience Certificates are offered, one for each sex. These classes have to be open to all breeds and, for a certificate to be awarded, the winner must not have dropped more than 10 points out of a possible 300. To obtain the title of

Ob Ch Melfricka Limelight (Sire Ch Camrose Fabius Tarquin, dam Melfricka Go-for-Gold) Owner Mrs A. Richmond. Breeder Mr F. Hathaway.

Obedience Champion a dog must win three certificates under three different judges or win the Kennel Club Obedience Championship at Crufts. To compete in this, a dog must have won a certificate during the preceding calendar year. You will gather that it is not an easy task to make up an Obedience Champion and it demands great dedication and many hours of patient work on the part of the handler.

Should you feel that you wish to enter this highly competitive pastime, I would advise that you contact the Kennel Club to obtain a copy of Regulations for Tests for Obedience Classes and, also, to ask them for the addresses of one or two of Obedience Clubs within your area. The Northern Golden Retriever Association, the Southern Golden Retriever Society and the Golden Retriever Club might well be able to assist you as well. All three put on Obedience Classes at one of their shows every year.

As far as I am aware, there is currently only one Golden Retriever Obedience Champion and that is Mrs A. Richmond's Obedience Champion Melfricka Limelight.

Agility tests, which I am sure many readers will have watched on television, have little in common with obedience although they require a high standard of training and a really bright exuberant dog. For entertainment value for the general public there can, however, be no comparison. Obedience has to be so precise that the dogs frequently show no real animation and, in watching such exercises as 'Down ten minutes, handler out of sight', it is hard to become truly partisan! Having said this, it in no way detracts from the achievement of the trainers nor the patience of their dogs.

Agility tests have been in existence for about ten years, the annual highlight of this growing sport being the Pedigree Chum Agility Stakes at the International Horse Show. One of its most endearing aspects is the speed and obvious enthusiasm of the participants, both human and canine. In 1983 the Agility Club was formed and now there are a number of clubs throughout the country from which you can obtain advice and help in training. The amount of equipment required makes it difficult to do much training at home, unless you are fortunate enough to have sufficient space and money to build your own course. Contact the Kennel Club to help you locate your nearest club and for up-to-date information on regulations.

Mr and Mrs S. Zingg's home-bred Ch Rayleas Callum. A truly dual purpose dog, for he is the only full champion in the breed, at the time of writing, with four field trial awards to his credit.

16

British Veterinary Association & Kennel Club Hereditary Eye Defects and Hip Dysplasia Schemes

When I originally wrote this book, some eleven years ago, I said that when buying a puppy it was essential that both parents had certificates, under the BVA/KC scheme for freedom from hereditary eye diseases, namely, Progressive Retinal Atrophy (PRA) and Hereditary Cataract (HC). As far as PRA is concerned I still maintain that this is paramount. However, such certificates can not be taken as a guarantee that at some future date, your puppy may not develop either of these conditions. It is very unlikely now that PRA will rear it's ugly head, for that has, to a very large extent, been eliminated, but, even after some 35 years of eye testing, hereditary cataract can still appear, possibly having skipped several generations, all of whom have certificates of freedom from this condition. When an ophthalmologist examines a dog he is giving his opinion at the time that he does this, his findings do not constitute either a Guarantee or a Warranty. However, the scheme has achieved much, introduces a reasonable degree of safety and, where a breeder has complied with the conditions of the scheme, he/she has utilized all that veterinary science has to offer to date.

There are two known forms of PRA, generalised and central, the latter is the one we have always been told affects Goldens. In this condition the retina, which is a thin membrane lining the interior of the eyeball, is first affected in the centre and then the condition slowly spreads outwards, causing peripheral vision. Total blindness is not inevitable with central PRA, as it is with generalised PRA, but, nevertheless, it is a major problem, particularly with a working dog. Twice I have seen Labradors out on a shoot, it quite easily could have been Goldens, turning their heads almost sideways to mark the fall of a bird, because their sight had nearly completely gone. Under no circumstances should a dog with PRA be bred from, however good it is. It is some 34 or 35 years since the first Golden eye testing session, conducted by Dr Keith Barnett, took place. This was at the GRC's Championship Show at Sandford, close to Oxford. Unfortunately there is no record of how many dogs were examined, but it is known that 25% failed for PRA, HC, or both. At that time the Irish Setters were having a terrible time with generalised PRA, frequently referred to as 'night blindness', but whatever name was used, the outcome was the same – total blindness. The condition, as in the case of Irish Setters, can frequently be diagnosed a few weeks after birth, whereas in some of the other breeds affected it may lie dormant for several years. Both forms constitute a disaster. Generalised PRA because it leads to certain blindness, and whilst in the case of central PRA this can equally be the case, often this does not occur until quite late in dog's life. The Irish Setter breeders adopted a very stringent policy of 'putting down' any affected puppies and, in some cases adults. Such a policy proved very rewarding as far as bringing the condition under control, although I understand that now, due to a more casual approach by some, this abnormality is again making itself known. It may well have been a case of a little knowledge being dangerous, and people thinking that all PRA was the same. A great friend of mine for many years made up two Golden Field Trial Champions in one season, both getting the 'second leg' to their title within three days of each other. He was elated. However, shortly after achieving this he took them both to have their eyes examined – both had PRA. He was completely shattered and had them both put down immediately; something he regretted for the remainder of his life. The dogs had central PRA and could have had many happy years, as someone's shooting companion, before their sight became so bad that they were unable to do their job.

Fortunately PRA is now very limited within the breed and does not constitute a major problem. There is no doubt that the BVA/KC scheme has been largely responsible for achieving this state of affairs. Alas, the same cannot be said about cataracts. There have now been thousands of Goldens examined under the scheme since its inception, but the amount of information amassed that is helpful to breeders in combating the ailment is negligible. The scheme operates on the basis of an annual examination of a dog's eyes by one the panel of the BVA approved ophthalmologists (appendix 2). A certificate is issued indicating whether a dog has failed or passed. The results are sent to the KC and, if it has failed, this is noted on the registration certificate of any puppies it may produce. The result of all official eye tests appears in The Kennel Club Breed Supplement. This was not always the case, for to begin with only the passes were made public, failures left unrecorded not for general scrutiny.

In 1984, it was agreed at the Annual Golden Retriever Breed Conference, to approach Dr Keith Barnett of the Animal Health

Trust with regard to carrying out further research into hereditary cataract. This he agreed to do in conjunction with Dr Roger Curtis, but only in respect to Goldens examined at the Animal Health Trust. A committee was formed with representatives from the various clubs, of which I had the honour of chairing. We met a number of times at the AHT, always with Dr Barnett, or Dr Curtis in attendance. Their research being limited to dogs examined at the AHT obviously narrowed the field greatly. There were, at that time, over thirty other ophthalmologists doing similar, if possibly not as many, individual examinations. The various Golden Retriever Clubs subscribed something in excess of £3,000 annually towards the research for a number of years.

Work started in January 1985. During the first eighteen months 1,141 Goldens were examined, of which 86, that is 7.5 per cent, were found to be affected with hereditary cataracts. This was a considerable improvement on the first eye-testing session carried out by Dr Barnett at the Club Show. From this stage onwards it seemed to me rather like digging a hole, the more one dug, the bigger the problem appeared to be, for it transpired there were a number of forms of hereditary cataract. Undoubtedly very interesting for the researchers, but, I would suggest, not a lot of help to the breeders. There is no doubt that constructive help is dependent upon such work and on new facts coming to light. Nevertheless, when one stops and considers the thousands of pounds paid by Golden Retriever owners over a period in excess of thirty years, it seems there is little they have received in return and little that the ophthalmologists can be certain about, except that the 'problem' is greater and more far reaching than was originally thought. For example, for years permanent certificates for freedom from PRA and HC were issued when a dog was 6 years old. It was subsequently established that both defects could appear years later – in fact after the end of a dog's breeding life. This must surely, to a great extent, negate the the full value of the scheme?

After thirty five years of eye testing there is no certainty that owners, after years of careful selective breeding of their dogs, may not find all their efforts shattered by the sudden appearance of HC in a line that was believed to be free. For example, a vet friend of mine, who has been most careful over checking both eyes and hips of her dogs, had a five year old Golden bitch with clear certificates from a year old and I'm almost certain the owner had bred a litter from her. When taking her bitch for her annual eye check she was devastated to be told that the bitch had HC, and yet for certainly two generations, probably more, her ancestors were clear.

One friend of mine who had done everything by the book from the time she started breeding Goldens, presented her dogs for their annual eye evaluation. She took her 8 year-old stud dog, who had received his permanent certificate of freedom from hereditary eye diseases two years earlier – at the age of 6 years. She only took him because the ophthalmologist concerned said he would like to see the older dogs, even after he had given their permanent certificate. Imagine her horror when she was informed that her much loved and, indeed, much used stud dog had failed on both conditions! Another eminent eye specialist was consulted and he confirmed both findings. Subsequently, a daughter of this dog, owned by the same lady, was found to have hereditary cataract at 8 years of age, the end of her breeding life. It is said that lightning never strikes in the same place twice; I don't think that this breeder would agree. She was only just beginning to get over the shock when next she presented some more of her dogs for their annual inspection. This time she took along another dog, 11$^1/_2$ years old, who had held his permanent certificate for five and a half years, but had still been looked at annually. He had retired from stud and really only went along for the ride. When he'd finished looking at the others the ophthalmologist said to the owner, 'Well, I'd better look at the old boy, otherwise he'll feel left out.' Minutes later she was told that the dog definitely had hereditary cataract. As with the first one, she sought a second opinion. Again the diagnosis was confirmed. Such happenings, whilst probably less frequent than they were, are by no means rare. I recently had a long telephone conversation with one of the country's most successful and highly respected breeders for over half a century or more, and she was talking to me about a dog of her's, a champion, who had failed his eye test for hereditary cataract when about 5$^1/_2$ years old. His forebears had, for a number of generations, clear certificates. She withdrew the dog from stud and made no secret as to the reason. Recently she received an enquiry from a knowledgeable breeder, could she use this dog at stud? The answer was in the affirmative, providing the person who wished to use him did not mind the registration certificates for the puppies showing he had failed under the BVA/KC eye scheme. The reply was that this was of no great importance, for if blindness did occur it would almost certainly be in old age and eyes were not the only factor that had to be taken into consideration when planning a mating.

Hereditary cataracts normally do not mean total blindness; in fact there must be hundreds of pet Goldens that are affected, but, because their owners seldom see any point in having their dogs' eyes checked, for the situation can't be altered, no one knows anything about them. Probably, as in years gone by, the owners think their pets' sight is failing a bit with old age; after all, ours often does, so why shouldn't a dog's? Unless you are a breeder, there is no reason to become over-concerned regarding hereditary cataracts. According to the textbooks, the commonest form is a small non-progressive opacity at the back of the lens. This is only visible with the aid of an ophthalmascope; it cannot be seen with the naked eye. Normally this does not progress or have an effect on vision. There is a progressive form but this, fortunately, is far less common. Do not form the impression that cataract is confined to Goldens. It is common in a number of breeds such as Afghan Hounds, American Cocker Spaniels, Boston Terriers, Cavalier King Charles Spaniels, German Shepherds, Labradors and a number of other breeds.

Readers might well get the impression that I do not attach too much importance to the eye scheme. Up to the end of 1997 they would have been wrong. It was, up to then, a useful, if far from infallible aid in planning a breeding programme and I was a strong supporter. However, in 1997 the BVA decided to transfer Goldens from schedule 3 of the official eye testing scheme to schedule 1, thus including Multifocal Retinal Dysplasia (MRD) and generalised PRA (the one which for years we were told did not affect Goldens). The decision to do this was based on finding about 120 dogs, out of somewhere in the region of 3,000 examined within the breed under the BVA/KC Eye Scheme, showing signs of retinal folds. The first question that one has to ask, bearing in mind that the existence of retinal folds has been known for a number of years, what harm do they do? According to the BVA, (this I have in writing from them) MRD has never as yet produced blindness in Goldens. It has always been said to be congenital, that is present at birth. The BVA say that the mode of inheritance is unknown, but it's presence could be identified by eye screening at 6 to 12 weeks and that it was believed to be hereditary. When the BVA decided to change the scheduling, in September of 1997, they notified The Kennel Club. However, the latter, did not bestir themselves to inform either the Breed Clubs, or the Breed Council until the 5th January 1998 – five days after the re-scheduling came into force! Several dogs, going for their annual eye check early in January, were immediately failed having previously held clear certificates. Failed for something which has, at the time of writing, never produced blindness or defective sight in Goldens. Just after the time the new scheduling came into being, one stud dog was taken for his annual check up. He already had three or four clear certificates from the ophthalmologist concerned, who failed him for MRD. There were four bitches at the time in-whelp to this dog. All whelped successfully and the four litters were examined under the BVA/KC Litter Screening Scheme for Congenital Hereditary Eye Defects. All passed except one, which the ophthalmologist did not fail but, at the time of writing, wishes to see again.

At a very conservative estimate there are anything between 125,000 and 150,000 Golden Retrievers in the country. I have enquired from a number of veterinary surgeons as to how many Goldens they have examined that were blind, or had defective eye sight, due to MRD? In all cases the answer has been 'none' of which they were aware. Yet the BVA/KC have, so it appears, gone a long way towards jeopardizing some thirty five years of work by breeders and owners, by moving the goalposts, changing the schedule to include MRD which, at the best, can only be described as a fringe condition, so far identified in probably something less than 0.009% of the Golden population of the country and, which as yet, has not been known to cause blindness. No wonder a lot of experienced breeders are saying they will boycott the scheme rather than have the stigma 'failed' applied to their dogs should it be found they have a retinal fold(s). Such breeders, however, have every intention of still having their dogs' eyes examined annually for PRA and HC, but outside the official scheme. The latter is entirely voluntary, but there are many who are overawed by The Kennel Club, and the mystique of the BVA and will passively accept whatever dictate these bodies may promote under the guise of breeding healthier dogs, irrespective of what may be lost in breed type, working ability and, above all temperament. I was recently told by a vet that there were 200 conditions and ailments in cats, 400 in dogs and 4,000 in humans. It is accepted that the latter can procreate without fear or hindrance, even when it is known that those involved are affected with a hereditary disease that could lead to death or disablement – it's known as human rights! Yes, the BVA/KC eye scheme is voluntary, but how volun-tary is 'voluntary' when the public are, in a number of cases, brainwashed by the general veterinary practitioner into believing that when buying a puppy, they must be sure that the parents have certificates for freedom from hereditary eye diseases and good hip scores, which, with the exception of PRA, are not, in the vast majority, going to bring about any problems which, in humans, would simply be compatible with old age. These tests should not be the main criteria when planning a breeding programme, purely aids, which is what they were originally intended to be.

To move on to the other half of the title to this chapter, 'hip dysplasia' – what is it? In layman's terms it is badly-fitting hip joint, occurring when the head of the femur, the thigh bone, is not correctly shaped and does not make a perfect union with the acetab-ulum, the hip socket. It is a subject that, over the years, has led to much controversy; even the vets do not agree. Around 1960 the BVA/KC Hip Dysplasia Scheme came into being. From the start, from a breeder/owner's point of view, it was unsatisfactory, at that stage simply because it supplied insufficient detail. There were three categories. First, there were those that came within the standard of normality and, for these, a certificate was issued to that effect. Second, there were those issued with what is described as a breeder's letter. Which said:

'The above dog, whose radiograph was recently submitted to the panel of scrutineers appointed by the BVA to assess films for hip dysplasia, shows borderline changes which place it outside the range of normality as agreed by the panel and so a certificate cannot be issued. Despite these findings, it may be felt necessary to utilise animals of this category for breeding purposes as in certain breeds, the incidence of hip dysplasia is sufficiently high that if all affected animals were withdrawn, the breed might become extinct or other inherited defects might be promoted because of the restriction.'

Third, there were those who received notification of failure. This did not say how bad the hips were and, therefore, only a very small percentage of breeders gave cognizance to the scheme. Thus it drifted along for nearly twenty years. In 1971, whilst my wife was away very seriously ill in hospital, I thought we should go with the 'tide' and so had all the Bryanstowns X-rayed. I remember our vet was really quite pleased with the results and sent off the plates to be scrutinised. A number of weeks passed, but nothing was heard, even-tually the vet telephoned. After some delay he was to be told they did not think they had received the X-rays, but, if they had, they must have lost them! Unfortunately the vet had not obtained a cer-tificate of posting, so that was the end of that. At least we'd tried!

In 1978, thanks to the persistence and hard work on the part of the geneticist, Dr Malcolm Willis, the BVA/German Shepherd Dog League (GSDL) hip scoring scheme came into being. Late in 1983 it was extended to other breeds. This was to prove far more enlightening, the hips being scored from 0 to 108, 54 each hip. The lower the score the better the hips. Translated into the terms of the old KC scheme, which still existed, normality was a score of 0 to 4, and a breeder's letter related to a score of 5 to 8.

I have often wondered at the term 'normality' because, from the evidence so far available from scoring, 0 to 4 is certainly not normal, at least in the accepted sense of the word. An eminent orthopaedic surgeon once said to me, 'You dog breeders are a strange lot. You expect your dogs to have identical hips, but we don't. You get all worked up if someone breeds from a dog that's a bit lame. Yet no one objects at the same thing happening to humans!' He certainly had a point.

As in the case of the eye scheme, I was full of enthusiasm when the BVA/GSDL's scheme was opened to other breeds and our Bryanstown kennel was one of the first to be scored. To be precise, X-rays of all the dogs in the kennel were submitted on 3rd August, 1983. This included one old lad in his thirteenth year, arthritis and all! The mean score for the entire kennel was 19, the lowest was 3. There is no doubt that breeders (not only in Goldens) owe much to Dr Willis for the work he has done and, indeed, is still doing, if for no other reason than that through his efforts, facts and figures have been and are continually becoming available. How much value these are to breeders I feel is debatable, at least as far as elimination of HD is concerned, if indeed it is possible to achieve this. However, in December 1986, some three years after Goldens had been allowed to participate in the BVA/GSDL's scheme, 3,456 had been scored. The scores for these covered a range of 0 to 104 and had a mean score of 18.47. Up to the 14th February, 1998 Dr Willis had assessed 17,462 Goldens, the mean score being 19.60. One is left asking what has been achieved after 15 years, with an increase in the mean score of 1.13? One has to accept that when an owner has a dog X-rayed and the hips are obviously going to have a high score, in many cases, these plates are not submitted. It is, therefore, probable that the mean score could be higher. It still leaves me wondering on what basis 'normality' was originally calculated?

Over a number of years attending talks by Dr Willis and, indeed, in the course of personal conversation with him, he has frequently said he would place hips about fourth in his order of importance when assessing the breeding potential of a dog. I fully agree. I also recall him saying, in the early days of hip scoring, that if an improvement of one percent could be made per annum in the mean score of a breed that would be about the most one could hope for. There is no doubt that temperament, breed type, working ability and eyes (even with all the failings in the scheme) should take precedence over hips. Further Dr Willis has frequently emphasised that if one has an outstanding bitch, possibly a Champion, with a high hip score and wish to breed from her, you should do so, but it is essential that if you do, you use a stud dog with a very low score.

Unfortunately, mating 0 to 0 does not ensure progeny with a score that might, in the past, have been described as 'normality', in fact it doesn't even ensure that they will come within the mean score. An experience of my own is typical. A number of years ago we bought a bitch puppy from one of the best known kennels in the history of the breed. The dam's score was 5, her half-brother, in the same kennel, was 10 and the sire's was quite acceptable. There were only two bitches in the litter, one we had, the other the breeder retained. At just over a year both were X-rayed and scored. The one retained by the owner had a score of 2, whilst her sister, who we had, was 54. Around the same time I had a young bitch, who was X-rayed as soon as she was old enough. Her score was 13. Her sire's score was 2, her dam's 7 and the grandam had a score of 3. I mention this just to illustrate that it will be a very long haul to reach a stage when so called 'normality' is the rule rather than the exception. One very experienced and knowledgeable breeder, about 13 or 14 years ago, brought a bitch with a total hip score of 9 to one of our stud dogs whose total score was 2. A dog puppy that the breeder particularly liked and intended keeping as a future stud dog went completely off his legs at $4\frac{1}{2}$ months and, when x-rayed it showed there was no connection whatsoever between the head of the femur and the acetabulum. She wrote, 'My vet did a muscle cutting operation immediately; it took five minutes and involved a three quarters of an inch incision and a stitch each side.' This is known as a Pectineus Resection. Her letter goes onto say that after three months of controlled exercise there was no more trouble. At just over a year she had him X-rayed and his hips scored – 53/53 = 106. The rest of the litter she told me were in the 20s. She goes on to say 'If it had been anyone else's litter I would have suspected too high protein and too much exercise. We never exercise pups – let them play about until they are 6 months.' The dog in question, so his owner said, could catch a running rabbit long after he'd have been eligible for veteran classes at championship shows. So much for breeding from a dog that could be categorized as 'normality' and a bitch just one point beyond this mythical figure.

There are veterinary surgeons who are far from convinced that hip dysplasia is entirely hereditary and think it can be caused by a number of factors. A few examples:- too much exercise when young, allowing puppies to spend a lot of time on their hind legs peering over a kennel wall and even running up and down stairs at an early age. There are others who cry 'hip dysplasia' immediately a dog is lame behind and those who say no dog should be bred if it hasn't a breeder's letter. I was even told of a lovely bitch spayed on a vet's advice, because her hips were not good enough to breed from, or so he said. She had a score of 5! Thankfully, whilst many vets these days have tunnel vision over the various schemes, there are few of that ilk around.

It would be a relatively simple task to fill a book with incidences which have occurred and which must throw doubt upon the viability of both hip and eye schemes. However, I will give one more example. Several years ago I was judging at a championship show in Germany. For those who are not au fait with the system of judging on the Continent, I will briefly explain. Normally there are not more than four classes, puppy, junior, open and champion. In each case one assesses a dog and dictates a critique to a secretary, grading the dogs excellent, very good and good. The latter implies it should not be bred from. The exhibitor receives a copy of the critique, in some countries before leaving the ring. Having assessed the class, the 'excellents' are brought back and placed as we would in this country. If there are not enough 'excellents', then the 'very goods' come in as well. At this particular show I was on junior, a dog came forward and before he was even stood up I knew at the best he was a 'good'; there really was nothing to like about him. His handler was attempting to 'top & tail' him, but was obviously very inexperienced and was making a right mess of it. With really no provocation at all the dog turned and bit his owner badly on the arm – there was blood everywhere. I sent both dog and handler out of the ring without a critique. When judging was over the owner returned, arm bandaged, saying that I had to do a critique on his dog. My secretary confirmed that this was so. Therefore, I did as asked. I don't remember exactly what I said, but I do remember saying the dog should never be used at stud. The owner was nearly crying with temper and frustration. He told me, with tremendous pride, that his dog had a hip score of 0–0, I believe he added that it was the only Golden in Germany with such a low score and there were numerous people waiting to use him at stud. I said, 'What about his temperament?' The owner shrugged his shoulders and replied, 'But he has the hips.' Personally, I would sooner have owned the dog with the score of 106, who had a wonderful temperament, and was sound for life after a minor operation. For many years, I don't know if they still adhere to the same policy, the Guide Dogs for the Blind Association did not make hips a major issue in their breeding policy. A very experienced breeder and judge of Goldens recently wrote to the BVA as follows, when they changed Goldens from schedule 3 to schedule 1 to include MRD. 'It does seem that these schemes have now become an academic exercise by the BVA, with no consideration for the dog as a whole and no consultation with breeders, who although have not the academic qualifications of the BVA, have the practical experience and although the BVA are not interested in the dog as a whole, we are going to nowhere unless there is communication between both parties.' How right she is. Having said that I would still recommend that dogs have their hips x-rayed and eyes examined for PRA and HC. However, having said this, in view of the fact that people frequently appear to seek compensation these days in all spheres of life if their purchase does not come up to their expectation, I would, if still breeding Golden Retrievers, institute 'Conditions of Sale', clearly stating the terms under which I was prepared to sell a puppy and would require the buyer to sign a paper to the effect that he/she was fully aware of the terms of the transaction.

It is incongruous to say the least, that the sale of goods legislation also applies to the sale of animals. How an inanimate object can be compared with a living creature can only be apparent to those who draft the laws under which we live. Further, the BVA and the KC have frequently declared the certificates issued under the BVA/KC Hereditary Eye Disease Scheme are purely an opinion and do not constitute a guarantee, similarly the same applies to the HD Scheme. For 'Conditions of Sale', such as I might adopt, see Appendix 5, however this is only for reference and before utilizing it should be checked by a member of the legal profession.

If something is not done soon to accept the true worth of the BVA/KC schemes and utilize the results in an intelligent way, namely as an aid, but by no means an infallible one, in formulating a breeding programme, then a time is going to come, if it has not already done so, when temperament, breed type and working ability are sacrificed on the alter of schemes that have proved, over a long period of time, to be flawed and lacking irrefutable scientific backing. The continuation along such a road is rapidly destroying the traditions and the very fabric of successful breeding, which most certainly does not mean just a fistful of certificates, for they are, so we are told by both the BVA and KC purely opinions, not a guarantee or lasting statement of fact.

Mrs Jenny Newton's home-bred Ch Coombstock Disco Dancer. Winner of 12 CCs & 2 Res: CCs, including BOB Crufts and Res: Gundog Group 1988

If this chapter has filled you with doubt and left you worrying, here are some reassurances. Dogs have their ailments as do humans, so get things in their right perspective. Think of the tens of thousands of Goldens and of course many other breeds, that undoubtedly do not have hips of 'normality', or even the 'mean score' and the many who almost certainly have hereditary cataract and the owners don't even know, or worry about it; yet they live to a ripe old age and have a happy and full life.

17

Idiopathic Epilepsy

It has been an accepted fact for many years that epilepsy occurs in dogs, as it does in humans and other animals. This is an area in which there can be a close liaison between the veterinary and medical professions in the methods of diagnosis, treatment and research. However, whereas epilepsy is accepted as a fact of life in humans and kept in the right perspective, this by no means applies when dogs are involved. It might help readers to achieve a balanced view if they stop to consider that, when I first published this book, in 1988, the Guide Dogs for the Blind did not take a dog out of service because of epilepsy, and furthermore, the police-dogs that suffered from it continued to work. As far as I am aware there has, rightly, been no change regarding this.

At the time of the original publication, an accepted leading authority on epilepsy in dogs, not only in this country, but through-out the world, was Dr Phyllis Croft, FRCVS who kindly agreed that I could quote her and, even better, declared that she would be happy to check what I had written – indeed a great honour. She first became interested in canine epilepsy as long ago as 1930. In 1944 she was awarded a PhD for her thesis on mental diseases. In 1950 she took up and virtually pioneered, electroencephalography as a means of studying epilepsy in animals and, subsequently, received the Livesey Medal for her work in this field. In 1959 she was made a Fellow of the Royal College of Veterinary Surgeons for her work on the subject. In 1975 she was invited to speak on epilepsy at the World Veterinary Congress. It is, therefore, not surprising, that after more than forty five years work she became recognised as one of the world's greatest authorities on the subject.

At the time I was fortunate enough to receive Dr Croft's help writing my book, what is now refered to as idiopathic epilepsy was normally characterized as primary epilepsy. However, the Department of Animal Neurology at the University of Berne, who have been doing extensive research into epilepsy in Goldens, use the term idiopathic, which broadly means a condition derived from an unknown or spontaneous cause and incorporates what at times have been refered to as hereditary, genuine, primary and functional epilepsy under this heading. In a paper by Dr P Srenk entitled 'Genetic fundamentals of idiopathic epilepsy in Golden Retrievers', it is stated that an estimated one percent of the world's dog population is affected by epilepsy. Dr Srenk also confirms what Dr Croft was saying many years ago, namely that sudden fits are by no means restricted to a genetic basis and can be caused by a number of circumstances and conditions. In the course of the work carried out at Bern it became apparent that dogs were more prone to idiopathic epilepsy than bitches. Much work went into the analysis of pedigrees and binomial testing which sustains the theory that there is an autosomal multifactorial recessive mode of inheritance, but this is really only a hypothesis and a truly ambitious test-mating programme would be required to define the exact mode of inheritance. This confirms Dr Croft's findings of a number of years ago which are referred to later in this chapter.

Idiopathic epilepsy is common to many breeds of dogs and usually appears first at from 1 to 3 years of age. It is not sparked off by another illness. In the simplest of terms, all animals can go into convulsions given sufficient stimulus. In some dogs the fit threshold is lower than in the majority, and fits, or epileptic seizures, occur much more readily in these. According to Dr Croft, it is possible that heredity plays some part, but as yet nothing is proven. IF epilepsy is a genetic problem, then the genes would have to be present in both parents of any affected progeny. Therefore one can view with some cynicism the rumours that point the finger at stud dogs only; you can make your own evaluation of those charges.

Fits nearly always occur when a dog is relaxed and so there is little or no risk of them happening at a show or when a dog is working. It is almost certainly more distressing for the owner than the dog if it has a fit. I base this comment on the fact that, for a number of years, I had on my staff an epileptic. He not infrequently had a fit. It was distressing to watch and, indeed, frightening for those who had not seen it before. After three to five minutes he would get up and, he assured me on a number of occasions, he would feel none the worse and would continue with his work. Eventually he married and had children, and there was no hue and cry! It would be quite possible for a dog that was kennelled to have a fit, or fits, at night and the owner never to be aware of it. At the time when I had a large boarding kennel, there were several regular boarders whom I was told had fits from time to time. On every visit their owners brought their Mysoline pills with them. On no occasion, over a number of years did we need them. All the dogs lived a happy, full life and died at a ripe old age. As with most things, there are exceptions to the rule. Very occasionally a dog will have fit after fit and if so it is imperative that you get it to your vet, or call one in at once. A dog may live for many years after such an attack, known as status epilepticus, providing the attack is dealt with quickly. Idiopathic epilepsy does not become more serious with age. If fits become more frequent, this is almost certainly due to the lowering of the fit threshold because of some condition not connected with the nervous system.

At a meeting I attended at which Dr Croft was the speaker, she expressed the opinion that as yet there was no evidence that proved idiopathic epilepsy to be hereditary. Further, she went on to say that it would be virtually impossible to establish this as a fact. The only way would be to take a hundred or so suspects and breed from these, building up to about one thousand dogs over a period of ten years. These would have to be watched day and night. Dr Croft was adamant that there is only one way of establishing if a dog is suffering from idiopathic epilepsy, and that is by an EEG. You may wonder what an EEG is. It is an electroencephalograph, a record of the rhythmical electrical activity of the brain. In lay terms this record is a chart produced by boosting the electrical discharges from a dog's brain. The procedure is neither harmful nor painful for the patient.

Epilepsy is a symptom, not a disease. There are a number of possible causes of fits in dogs as, indeed, there are in other animals. Some examples are as follows:

Brain damage caused before birth. This can happen if a bitch suffers a body blow, or if she squeezes through a door or fence.
Brain damage at birth, due to injury caused at whelping.
Distemper, even if a dog has never shown any signs of the disease.
Vaccination against distemper. It has been verified by many veterinary surgeons that the vaccine can produce protein shock, which in turn may produce fits.
Injury. A dog could be hit by a car or have some other accident and appear perfectly all right at first, but start having fits as a result a year or more later.
Poisoning. This is not a major cause, but one that is quite possible, slug pellets being one form of poisoning that can produce fits.
Brain tumours. Fits from this cause would be most likely from 5 to 6 years of age onwards, although tumours can be the cause of fits at an earlier age.

Incorrect feeding. This is not as common now as in the past, although some foods are suspect because of bleaching, colouring agents, preservatives and other additives.
Toxaemia. The liver and kidneys are vital in maintaining the correct metabolism within the body. Should either the liver or kidneys be impaired, causing toxaemia, epilepsy can be an added complication.

These are just some of the possible causes of fits in dogs. At the meeting to which I have referred there were two very experienced veterinary surgeons present, both of whom said that they could think of at least fifteen or sixteen causes for fits in dogs, and those fits are commonly categorised as epilepsy.

Dr Croft stated that her findings were based on the examination of some 20,000 dogs. Surely they are more reliable as a basis for assessment than pure speculation that has no veterinary backing? Dr Croft further informed the meeting that epilepsy was no more frequent than in the past. Her advice to breeders was not to breed from a dog that definitely had primary epilepsy and not to mate

Mr & Mrs M. Gaffney's Ch & Ir Ch Galalith Crown Prince of Tyroll. BOB Crufts 1994 Winner 5 CCs, each time going BOB, plus 14 Green Stars under IKC rules. Photographed at 9 years.

Mr & Mrs B. Wilkinson's Sh Ch Tulliallan Bradley. Winner of 5 CCs & 1 Res: CC, including BOB Crufts & 4th Gundog Group 1997.

again a dog and a bitch that had definitely produced epilepsy; however, if both dog and bitch were particularly good there was no reason why they should not each be mated again but to a DIFFERENT partner. Finally, I must repeat what I have already said, which is that like a number of other problems epilepsy must be considered in the right perspective. As Dr Croft wrote in a letter to me, 'I don't think I've ever known a subject which generated such a lot of bizarre rumours as epilepsy.' For those seeking further information on this subject, I strongly recommend Dr Croft's book (see Appendix 1).

It would seem that the research into idiopathic epilepsy carried out at the Institute of Animal Neurology in Berne from 1988 to 1995 gives every appearance of being more far reaching than that done in this country over the same period. Further, they have reverted to the use of electroencephalography for confirmation of idiopathic epilepsy, as used by Dr Croft and subsequently belittled by some neurologists in this country as being ineffective!

18

Full Circle – Breeding from your Golden

By the time your boy or, indeed girl has reached the age of 18 months to 2 years, you may well have developed such a love for Golden Retrievers that you will want to start breeding them. If your dog is a male, he must have had fairly spectacular success in the show ring or field trials for you, as a one-dog owner and a newcomer, to receive any great demand for his services at stud. If he is going to be used, he really should have a bitch at around a year old to get him started but, unless you feel fairly sure that there is going to be a reasonable demand for him, I would think twice before embarking along this road. Much depends upon your circumstances. There is a risk that having wetted his appetite he will go wandering off at every opportunity looking for new conquests. Secondly, and far more important, it is not as easy as you might think to have a dog at stud and, unless you have an experienced person to help to begin with, you could be in for an awful lot of hassle!

Well over 50 per cent of bitch owners have very little idea of when a bitch is ready for mating. Most seem to want to come on the eleventh day, largely because, knowing nothing, they have asked their vet, the eleventh day seems very popular with vets! When this happens and the bitch is not ready, frequently I am reminded of something that I heard as a boy, 'Vets are excellent doctors but poor stockmen.' Unless they happen to breed dogs, they know only the theory and, from the practical aspect, are often no more knowledgeable than the owner of the bitch. There is no hard and fast rule. I have had a bitch mate happily on her eighth day and go in-whelp. Another I tried from the twelfth day and it was not until the twenty-second day that we got a mating; she had thirteen puppies! The bitch that mated on the eighth day had three litters in all: the second time the twelfth and thirteenth were the optimum days and the last time it was the seventeenth and eighteenth. On the sixteenth day she would have nothing to do with the dog and the same applied on the nineteenth: she just didn't want to know. By the twenty-second day she was completely out of season and running around in the exercise paddock with three stud dogs,

175

including the one that mated her, plus a number of bitches, none of whom paid the slightest attention to her. Recently I was involved with the mating of a bitch that started off with quite a normal season. On the thirteenth day, although she was still discharging, showing colour, she was tried but would not have the dog near her. This was the case every day from then until the eighteenth day, when she was mated, but only because the stud dog was very forceful and experienced. Certainly there was no co-operation on her part. She continued in season. On the twenty-fifth day she stopped showing colour and mated quite happily, and this happened again on the twenty-seventh day; she had a lovely litter!

As I have said, there are no hard and fast rules, only guidelines. These examples are indeed exceptions, but if you have a stud dog, you will have to cope with exceptions and know what's what. Frequently, the normally sweet, loving pet becomes a tigress when taken to be mated. You may well have to tie her mouth up to stop her from biting and you could need several helpers to hold her. Incidentally, the fewer strange people there are around the better. On many occasions when a bitch has arrived, mum, dad and a horde of kids have all come along for the party; all are quite put out when told that only one member of the family can be present and that the occasion is not an opportunity for a sex lesson! A bitch that has been really difficult to get mated will relax once she is mated, will enjoy the experience and in due time become a really good mother. It is vital that you do not let a bitch snap at or actually bite a young dog. Should this happen it could put him off for life. Even some experienced dogs become very hesitant if a bitch growls a lot. You should be able to guide and help your dog and to do this you will want him to get used to your touching his more intimate parts. If you do this from an early age you should have no trouble later. If you don't do that, when the time comes to do it he might well object. Many years ago I had a stud dog and in no way would he let me help him, nor would he have anyone holding the bitch. This caused more than one problem and I vowed that it was one I'd never have again. There will be those who say, 'Why not let him just run around and let nature take its course? If the bitch got out she'd probably mate quite happily with some mongrel.' True enough, but she would only mate when she was ready and, under such circumstances, no one would know how many dogs she had 'taken the face off' before deciding the time was right.

Every stud dog owner has their own way of working their dog. This may well have to differ from dog to dog; all are individuals.

This is not something for which you can give a precise formula and there is no doubt that practical experience is the best teacher. When possible, I like there to be three people present when mating a bitch, one of them holding her, which can be an arduous and back-breaking task. However, there is no reason to get a crick in your back; holding the bitch is much easier if you sit on an old chair. You can then have her head in your lap and, should she get troublesome, you can clamp her shoulders between your knees. Another person is required, if it can be arranged, to kneel by the bitch, keeping her tail out of the way by holding it round to the side. This person can also help to keep her on her feet should she try to sit down. The third, and most important person works the stud dog. This entails pushing the vulva forward and guiding the dog. A lubricant, such as Vaseline, is normally used. When the dog has entered the bitch, as he finishes ejaculating the person working him puts an arm around behind the dog to hold him, and virtually at the same time, moves to get a knee in place to help keep him there, in case the bitch does not let him enter far enough to tie. It is natural for a dog to turn once tied, so that they are tail to tail. However, many stud dog owners, including myself, do not let their dogs do this, chiefly in case the dog should hurt himself. Instead they let the dog slide off and stand beside the bitch, then hold the couple together until they wish to part. Normally a tie will last from fifteen to twenty minutes, but it can at times be up to two hours or even more. Fortunately, this doesn't happen often, but when it does it becomes a long and boring pastime and there is nothing that I know of that will part them. You've just got to sit it out! A tie is not essential for a successful mating, it's just the icing on the cake for the dogs. I have known of dogs that have not tied once during their entire breeding life. I have had a number of cases where a dog has entered a bitch, ejaculated and been off her within seconds, yet the bitch has gone in-whelp. However, I always feel happier if there is a tie as I think that a bitch is more likely to ovulate then. If you have a good mating but decide to try again, do that after forty-eight hours; the sperm will live in the bitch for approximately that length of time. If she is no longer interested, so much the better. Almost invariably, it has been my experience, if a bitch goes off quickly she will be in-whelp.

If your Golden is a bitch and you decide to breed from her, don't make this something you decide on the spur of the moment. Give the matter a lot of careful thought. Apart from anything else, consider the time that is required to rear a litter. It is an exacting job. First, make sure her eyes are all right and have them examined under the BVA/Kennel Club scheme. Whilst this still leaves much to be desired, it is the best safeguard that we have. No reputable stud dog owner will accept a bitch for mating without a current eye certificate. Don't breed from your bitch just for the sake of breeding a litter and don't breed from her if she has a major fault. Only do so if your bitch is of good quality and temperament, the latter being the most important thing. Don't breed from her because of the old wives' tales, often subscribed to by vets, that it is good and necessary for the bitch's well-being. Rubbish! She may become more mature, certainly, but that is all. I have known many top-class working bitches that were never bred from, had lovely temperaments and were shot over until 10 or 11 years of age or even older. To carry the argument that each bitch should have a litter to its logical conclusion, one might as well say every mare should have a foal or, for that matter, every woman should have a baby!

The question of hips is a matter of personal choice; there are many more important aspects to take into consideration. I have every bitch I breed from these days X-rayed and scored and I would recommend that you do the same, if only as a public relations exercise. As I have already said, if this is done in conjunction with other safeguards, then a breeder has taken all possible steps towards producing sound, healthy puppies.

Once you have satisfied yourself regarding the above, the next thing to do is to study your bitch's pedigree and decide what dog will tie in with her breeding. Don't just use any old dog, such as the one down the road because it happens to be near! If that is your approach, then it is better for the breed if you forget the whole idea. You should line breed to perpetuate the good and outstanding points of your girl's forebears and to retain breed type. Years ago, when I was very involved in Jersey cattle it was customary, particularly on the island of Jersey itself, to mate grandfather to grandaughter and grandson to grandmother. This produced some wonderful animals and I have seen this same principle applied to Goldens with great success. However, don't get too close such as half-brother and half-sister. Decide what dogs you like, study their pedigrees and see how they fit in with that of your bitch. Seek advice; most experienced breeders will be glad to help. You are likely to be more successful if you keep to the blood lines you already have. This is presupposing that you have a well-made bitch of good established breeding. Don't go off at a tangent and choose a totally unrelated dog just because, say, he won at Crufts. You might be lucky, but there again the chances are that you might not – stick to the line you know and favour.

If you are going to breed, I strongly advise breeding from your bitch at 18 months to 2 years. This in all probability would be her third season. My experience has been that the longer you leave it the more difficulty you will have in getting your bitch in-whelp. On this basis, if you so wish, you can breed certainly three and possibly four litters. I do not believe in breeding from a bitch after she is 6 years old and that, for the first litter, would be leaving it very late. It is like a woman having her first baby when she is aged 42; it is quite possible but not very practical!

Usually, once a bitch has had two seasons, a pattern is established and you can plan ahead and make provisional arrangements with the owner of the stud dog. A normal season is twenty-one days and, if you are proposing to breed from your bitch, it is most important to make sure that you note down the first day. This is not always easy; some bitches lick themselves clean and it is difficult to spot that they are showing colour. A week or so before the bitch comes into season she will urinate far more frequently than normal; when this happens, keep a close watch on her. If you have any doubts, swab her. This can easily be done by inserting into the vagina a cotton-bud, such as is used for cleaning babies' ears. If this shows a pink stain, then you will know that she is in season. As a bitch gets nearer to the time for mating, the vulva enlarges and then softens. One indication that a bitch is reaching the optimum time is what happens when you gently scratch her beside the root of her tail. If she turns it to one side, she should soon be ready. This is not infallible, but it is a help. Another thing to do – and you cannot be squeamish over these matters if you want to be successful – is to scrub your hands and, with the aid of a little Vaseline, insert a finger up her vagina. If she is very tight and perhaps squeaks, you are too early. Such preliminaries could save you many miles of unnecessary motoring should your selected stud dog be some distance away. You must be there on the right day; that is, when the bitch is receptive and ovulating. Regarding the latter, I have found that a 2 ml injection of Receptol, given one hour before mating, is helpful in getting bitches in-whelp. Obviously, if you have a journey of some hours to the stud dog this cannot be administered by your vet. You will, therefore have to obtain it from him in those circumstances and inject your bitch about one hour before reaching your destination. Some owners use a test tape, obtainable from chemists, to ascertain the glucose level in the vagina, which is considerably increased at the time of ovulation I have never done this, preferring to rely on normal physical signs and examination.

When you feel that the time is nearly right, contact the stud dog owner and arrange a suitable time for you both. Do not forget to take both the eye and registration certificates with you. Most stud dog owners will wish to see these before mating a bitch. In their turn they should show you their dog's certificate and, if he's been X-rayed, his hip score. If these are not forthcoming, ask to see them. When you arrive at your destination, do not let your bitch out of the car until told to do so. Before introducing her to the dog let her have a run and empty herself.

Some stud dog owners insist on tying a bitch's mouth up or muzzling her, usually the former. To do this one can use either a length of bandage or an old tie. When necessary I use the latter. Make a loop with a single knot, place the loop over the muzzle and with the knot on top pull tight. Cross the two ends under the bottom jaw and take the ends back behind the ears. Fasten it with a bow for quick release. Don't become disturbed if this is done; it is necessary for the safety of the stud dog and, indeed, protects the hands of the person holding the bitch – quite likely yours! Once the mating occurs, you can take the tie off and just hold the bitch quietly until they part. Immediately the mating is over return your bitch to the car. Do not let her urinate.

You pay the stud fee at the time of mating. You should receive a copy of the dog's pedigree – usually five generations – and a stud receipt. I always give a copy of the dog's hip scoring sheet. On the stud receipt any special arrangements should be noted. It is customary, but not obligatory, within the next twelve months for a free mating to be given if the bitch does not go in-whelp. It should be noted that this mating is to the SAME bitch and not to any other that the owner may have. When you arrive home, be sure to keep your girl away from any other dogs, that is, in the male sense. The fact that she has been mated will not necessarily stop her from doing so again!

Regarding the general care of your bitch during pregnancy, the gestation period is sixty-three days. Treat her the same as before mating, with one exception: the addition of calcium to her diet. You can buy this in various forms, sometimes with fancy names and at quite ridiculous prices. I have found that calcium lactate, obtainable from Boots, provides all that is required. Four tablets a day are sufficient; more than that is just waste and will not be absorbed by the bitch. These days there are a host of additives that one can buy for pregnant bitches, but normally they should not be necessary.

It is difficult to be certain that a bitch is in-whelp until about three weeks before she is due; even then it is not always possible. Some bitches carry their puppies very high up in the uterus and, with a small litter, it can be hard to be absolutely positive. Not many years ago I had a big-bodied bitch who was mated and, just days before she was due, showed no signs of being in-whelp. She was due on a Wednesday; I had to call at the vet's on the Monday and took her with me. I asked my vet friend to examine her, and he pronounced that she was not in-whelp. When I returned home I left her in the kennel she shared with another bitch and one of the stud dogs. On the Wednesday afternoon I was busy in the garden, and suddenly I heard squealing coming from the kennels. At the time we had a plague of baby rabbits around the place and I thought that one had got through the chain-link fencing into the kennel. I ran across and found the bitch who had not been mated carrying a newly born puppy in her mouth, whilst the stud dog and mother looked on! I called my kennelmaid and we moved the bitch and her puppy, a dog, into the whelping kennel. Having seen them safely settled, and the puppy sucking away contentedly, I went into the house. Some forty minutes later I went back and asked the kennelmaid if 'the Lone Ranger' was all right. 'Yes', came the reply, 'So are his two sisters!' Three puppies had arrived in under an hour and all were massive. Forty-eight hours earlier a very experienced veterinary surgeon had confirmed my opinion, namely that the bitch was not in-whelp! How wrong one can be! However, this was an exception, for normally there is little doubt, but it does emphasise the fact that you must always be vigilant.

It is important to keep your girl well exercised and not to let her become over-fat; feed her normally. Occasionally a bitch will go off her feed at around three weeks for a few days. This phase quickly passes. Should this happen, frequently afterwards the bitch will appear to be ravenous, but stick to your normal feeding. At three weeks, or thereabouts, it is possible for a veterinary surgeon or, indeed, an experienced lay person, to feel the fertilised eggs before they are drawn up higher into the uterus. At this stage they are about the size of a small marble. I always consider three to four and a half weeks a critical period when a bitch may well reabsorb: that happens when the fertilised eggs virtually dissolve and are absorbed by the bitch. In these circumstances there is no discharge, such as one would see if a bitch were to abort. Should your bitch reabsorb – and it can happen without your knowing it – there is no reason why the next season she should not go in-whelp and carry her puppies the full time.

As the pregnancy advances, it is important to keep up the exercise, but not to the extent of over-tiring the bitch. At around five weeks the teats may become enlarged and pink. This is a useful guide that a bitch is in-whelp, but it is by no means infallible. Between five and six weeks I start to increase the protein in the diet. If feeding a complete food, as I do, start adding meat, working up to about ¾ lb per day. If you feed biscuit and meat, then your bitch should be getting 1½ to 1¾ lb of meat per day. Do not increase the carbohydrates. From seven weeks onwards, it is advisable to split her feed into two, giving half at night and half in the morning. An egg in a pint of milk at midday during the last week is a useful addition.

Make sure that your whelping kennel, or whatever facilities you are arranging, is ready three or four days before the puppies are due. A bitch who is having her first litter can easily be a couple of days early. Conversely, one that has had several litters can be two or three days late. Whether your choice is in the house or a kennel, the requirements remain much the same. The first essential is a whelping box, as shown in the diagram. Sufficient room is required without having it so large that the puppies get away from the bitch. Over the years I have tried a variation in sizes and have found that a box 3 ft 9 in × 2 ft 8 in with sides 1 ft 6 in high is ideal. The front should be individual boards, dropping into slots, so that the height can be raised as the puppies become older and more agile. A rail some 4½ in from the three sides and the same height from the floor is a safeguard against the puppies being lain on by the bitch. I make this so it can be quickly and easily put in place. I do not do this until the bitch has finished whelping. Again, after some trial and error, I have found that the best rail can be made from broom handles, halved and bolted together. The ends drop into wooden cups at the back and on each side. At the front the sides of the whelping-box and the rail are drilled, so that the latter can be held in place by a ⅜ in carriage bolt, blocked out the required distance from the sides with a piece of ½ in copper piping. This has the advantage that the rail can be put in place in a matter of three or four minutes and can easily be removed when the puppies are well on their feet and running around.

There are breeders of the old school who claim that heating is an unnecessary luxury and that a bitch should be able to generate all the heat that is required. Strictly speaking, as far as survival is concerned, this is correct. However, in cold weather, puppies that have additional heating thrive much better than those that don't. To provide this in a kennel a 275-watt infra-red bulb is quite adequate. This should be controlled by a thermostat so as to maintain a level temperature: 18°C (65°F) is comfortable for the bitch and warm enough for the puppies. Make it too hot and the bitch will be restless and may not remain quietly with her puppies. The bulb should be at least 3 ft 6 in above the bed. I have a division 2 ft 6 in high that drops into slots on either side of the kennel; this is so that the bitch can get away from the puppies when they become older. I have tried, and do not like, a lid or top that can be put over the whelping-box so that the bitch can jump up out of the way. If one has such an arrangement, when the top is in use the infra-red lamp cannot be used for the puppies. When the time comes for the bitch to want to be away from her pups, that is the time they most require the heat!

I always whelp bitches on newspaper. It is absorbent and can quickly and easily be changed. Once the bitch has whelped and been cleaned up I move her and the puppies on to a Vet-bed, or its equivalent, this is usually after twenty-four to thirty-six hours. It is remarkable how mobile the puppies become on this kind of surface.

A day or two before your bitch is due, make sure you have everything ready in the kennel. Don't forget to check that your infra-red heater, thermostat and light are all working. Spread newspaper in the box and have a good supply available to replace this. The bitch will shred it whilst 'nesting' prior to whelping, and it will become wet and soiled when she is whelping: necessitating frequent changing. You require a reel of thread and a pair of veterinary scissors. Those are to tie and cut the umbilical cord if necessary. You also need a small bowl, a bottle of Dettol (diluted and ready for use), cotton wool, several small towels, a cardboard box and a lead. In addition, have ready a folding garden chair and a small table, if there is room for the latter. Many years ago I took the advice I found in a text-book to include a small bottle of brandy in case the bitch or a puppy might require reviving. I have to date, I am glad to say, never required it for its designated purpose, but on a bitterly cold winter night around 3.00 a.m. I have found it to be a very positive adjunct to my equipment! In addition to the above, I always have a hypodermic syringe and a small quantity of pituitarin to stimulate contraction if necessary. However, it would be extremely unwise for an inexperienced person to use this, assuming even that they could obtain it. If your bitch has reached a stage of inertia, which is when such an injection would be warranted,

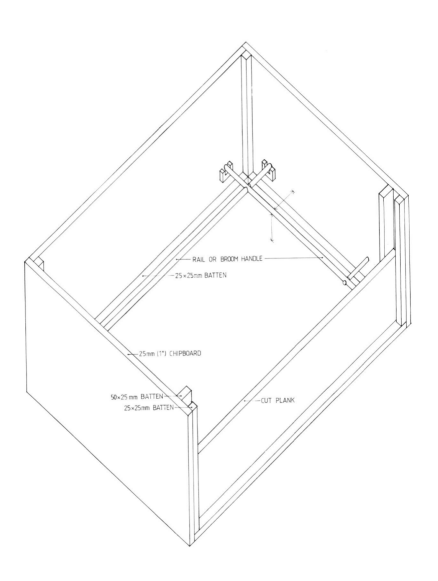

RAIL OR BROOM HANDLE

25×25mm BATTEN

25mm (1") CHIPBOARD

50×25 mm BATTEN

25×25mm BATTEN

CUT PLANK

Whelping Box

then it is time to call your vet. It is advisable to contact your vet anyway before your bitch starts to whelp, particularly in the case of a partnership, to ascertain who will be on duty at night should you require help in a hurry. However, Goldens are little trouble to whelp and, normally, you should have no problems.

The first sign that whelping is imminent is the bitch's lack of interest in food but, here again, there is no hard and fast rule. I once had a bitch that cleared up her food with great gusto at 4.00 p.m. When I went to look at her at 7.30 p.m. she had two puppies! This, however, is exceptional, but it is the exceptions that you must watch for. If and when your girl goes off her food, take her temperature. The normal temperature is 101.5°F; when a bitch is about to whelp her temperature will drop by two or three degrees. When this happens prepare for a night up. Very occasionally, one is lucky and a bitch will decide to whelp in the day, but about eight times out of ten they will choose the night. The ones I really like are those that keep one up all night and produce the first puppy at around 7.30 a.m!

The early stages of parturition is one of dilation. This can be of various lengths – it could last for two to three hours or for twenty hours, and sometimes it is even longer. The bitch is agitated and 'nests', that is, scrabbles up the newspaper and tears it into shreds. As she gets nearer to her time she will pant a lot and then sit quietly with a glazed look in the eyes. Finally, she will start contractions. To begin with, these are mild. The time of the first one should be noted. The length of time required for a puppy to be born is unpredictable. I have known a bitch to have four or five contractions and then a puppy has arrived. She can, however, go on straining for several hours before anything happens. If the bitch has been in labour for two and a half to three hours without any result, then it is time to have a talk with your vet.

The puppy arrives in a membrane and is attached by the umbilical cord to the afterbirth, or, to give it its correct name, the placenta. Everything should come away virtually together. In the majority of cases the puppies arrive head first but sometimes there is breech birth, that is, hindquarters first. If this happens, there is a greater chance that the membrane will rupture before the puppy arrives. Should this be the case, the puppy can be born minus its 'packing'. It is important to note whether the afterbirth comes away from the bitch; if retained it can lead to a lot of trouble. There are times, particularly with a big puppy, when a bitch needs some help. If this becomes necessary insert two fingers, having first dipped them in Dettol, over the puppy's head and exert a gentle downward pressure, that is towards the hocks, as the bitch strains. As soon as the puppy is born it is important to break the membrane, so that liquid escapes and the puppy can breathe. If it has difficulty in doing this, hold it up by the hindquarters, head down, and swing it gently to drain any fluid from it. If it still has difficulty, open its mouth and blow down its throat. Then take it in a towel and rub it briskly. Once it is breathing properly, it is time to put it up to the bitch's head so she can lick it and bite through the cord. The licking stimulates the puppy and helps with its respiration. If she does not sever the cord, tie it tightly with a piece of thread about one inch from the puppy's tummy then, first dipping the scissors in the Dettol solution, cut the cord. It is quite natural for the bitch to lap up the fluid and, disgusting as it may seem, for her to eat the afterbirth. It is equally natural for her to clean up the motions from the puppies for the first three or four weeks, or even longer.

Very occasionally a bitch will take no interest in her first puppy and appears completely bemused by the whole happening. When that occurs, having cut the cord and dried the puppy, hold it up to her and encourage her to lick it. If she still does not respond, move the puppy around to 'the milk bar' and get it latched on to a teat. This can necessitate drawing off a little milk with finger and thumb, really to wet the teat, then gently opening the puppy's mouth and putting the teat in it. Once the puppy starts to suck, the bitch will almost certainly take an interest.

If there is a breech birth and the membrane breaks before the puppy is born, it is essential to extract the puppy as quickly as possible as there is a very real danger of suffocation. Do not pull the puppy by its legs. Again, insert two fingers, this time over the hips, and draw gently but firmly downwards, not necessarily waiting for the bitch to have a contraction. As soon as it is free from the afterbirth, check to see how much life the puppy has in it. If it seems dead or nearly so, go through the procedure already described. This could be a time for two or three drops of brandy on the tongue – the puppy's! Should it seem very limp and lifeless and not respond to being briskly rubbed with a towel, try heat. If you happen to have an Aga, place the puppy on a towel in the bottom oven with the door open for five or ten minutes. Over the years I have revived quite a few 'dead' puppies in this way. If you haven't an Aga, then a hot-water-bottle will do. Once the puppy has recovered, get it back to mum and on to the milk bar as soon as possible. Normally, unless a puppy is a weakling, it achieves this without any help. After fifty years it still fascinates me to watch such a puny little creature make its way unhesitatingly to the source of nourishment.

Once the bitch has produced one puppy, two or three more are likely to appear in quick succession. The bitch will then rest for a while. After each birth I ease up her hindquarters and place some dry paper under her. When the bitch has had three or four puppies it is a good time to give her a drink of warm milk with a teaspoonful of glucose in it. As the litter increases in numbers, when another birth is imminent move the puppies already born to one side. If you don't do this, they will be caught in the flood and you will be repeatedly drying them. It is impossible to say how long it will take for a bitch to have her litter. The quickest I ever remember was eleven in an hour and fifty minutes; the longest was three in seventeen hours. It is difficult, even with years of experience, to be absolutely sure when a bitch has finished. She may keep having a contraction every fifteen or twenty minutes for several hours after the last puppy has arrived. This could be another puppy, but unless the intervals between the contractions become more regular, it is likely that she has retained an afterbirth, or the contractions could be due to soreness and general discomfort. For many years now I have made a point of getting my vet out within twelve hours of the last birth to check the bitch. As a routine thing they get a shot of pituitarin and antibiotic. The former will cause the bitch to expel any matter that has been retained in the uterus, which will happen within twenty minutes to half an hour after she has had the injection. It is important that the injection is given before the expiration of twenty-four hours after whelping. After that the cervix closes and anything left in the womb can cause serious trouble. Quite possibly an operation will be needed to remove whatever is in there and, in extreme cases, death can result.

When your bitch had had four or five puppies – much depends on how long she has been in labour – put the puppies into the cardboard box, slip a lead on your girl and take her out to 'spend a penny'. She won't be keen to leave her puppies, but it is necessary. When you return, leave her in the outer run of the kennel and quickly change the paper completely. Then let her in. Make sure she is in the whelping-box and sitting down before returning a puppy. Then, when she has this to distract her from the rest, gently pull her front legs out so she is lying down and give her the rest of the puppies as quickly as possible. The whole operation should not take more than about five minutes. Incidentally, you will have to keep her on the lead whilst you are out, otherwise you will achieve nothing as she will be frantically trying to get back to her babies.

When you feel reasonably certain she has finished, give her another drink of warm milk and glucose. Take her out again, going through the same routine as before, only this time when you return to the kennel give her hindquarters a good towelling. Settle her down with her puppies and always see that the smallest are safely latched on before putting the whole litter back. At this stage remain with the bitch for another twenty minutes or so. When you feel she is quite settled and the puppies are all full and happily suck-ling, leave her to rest. The milk produced at this early stage is known as colostrum and, for about the first thirty-six to forty-eight hours, contains the antibodies against such diseases as parvo virus and distemper, which makes it essential for the puppies.

Once the bitch has rested and been checked by the vet, clean her up. This is more easily and quickly done with a helper as she will be fussing to return to her babies. Shampoo her tail and hindquarters, then dry them thoroughly. Take the paper out of the whelping-box and wipe it out with Dettol. Having done this, spread some more paper – two or three sheets thickness – and a Vet-bed. You should keep newspaper under the latter for the whole time that it is in use. When the puppies urinate the liquid quickly passes through the Vet-bed and something is required to absorb it under-neath. You will need to change this paper twice a day when the puppies reach the age of about ten days onwards. Don't be surprised if there is some small amount of discharge from the bitch for two to three weeks after whelping. However, if this, after several days, remains dark, thick and somewhat smelly, contact your vet. That should not happen if you've taken the precautions I have already mentioned. Your bitch's motions for the first two to three days after whelping will be loose and black, but they should return to normal after that.

It is most important to make sure that all teats are being suckled and that the mammary glands are not hardening. This can some-times happen due to the bitch lying in an awkward position so that the puppies are unable to reach one or more of the teats. Examine your girl, when you have her out, night and morning. If any section seems very full make sure the biggest and strongest pup is latched on to the teat to suck it out. If a gland become hard, then strip some of the milk off by hand. If it feels hot and inflamed, foment the area with hot water four to six times a day, for five to ten minutes each time. Strip off as much milk as you can. Should the milk become thick and pussy in appearance it is time to call in your vet for, in addition to what you are already doing, your girl needs a course of antibiotics as she is starting mastitis.

It is important that the bitch has a high liquid intake to produce all the milk she will require for her brood. Water, of course, should always be available. In addition, give her a pint to a pint and a half of rather dilute milk, made up from a milk powder as already mentioned in an early chapter, at noon and again around 10.00 to 11.00 p.m. The reason for not mixing it to full strength, as would be required for the puppies, is that with the additional feeding she will be receiving it would almost certainly be too much for her and her motions would become excessively loose. For the first three to four days after whelping, keep her feeds on the small side, then work up to capacity – that is, to a quantity that she can take without upsetting her tummy. There are numerous excellent complete foods on the market today, but for over 20 years I have used the products of Roger Skinner Ltd (Appendix 1) and have found them to be excellent and economical. Further, they will send a rep to fully advise, if asked, as to which of their products you should use.

Once your girl has recovered from whelping, which will be in a remarkably short time, you will think there is nothing to this puppy breeding. All you have to do is watch and see they are full and contented, take the bitch out at regular intervals and feed her. Should any particular puppy never seem quite as full as the rest, when you put them back with mother see that it has a head start over the others. To do this you will have to stay with her for a few minutes before finally returning all the pack and you may well have to restrain her gently until they are all back. When the puppies are full and sleeping, it is normal for them to twitch. That is not, as I was once told in Belgium, a sign of epilepsy! By the time the pups are a week old, their nails will have grown and become very sharp. It is necessary to cut these about every week whilst the puppies are suckling. If it is not done, the bitch become positively lacerated from the needle-sharp claws, kneeding her glands as they suckle. At this age the nails can be cut with a sharp pair of scissors; there is no fear of splitting them when the puppies are so young.

Should the bitch have insufficient milk, or a very large litter, it may be necessary to give supplementary feeding every three hours. Providing the puppies are doing well, they can go for a six-hour period in the night without extra feeding. You can buy suitable bottles and teats from any good pet shop for this purpose. There are a variety of milk supplements available.

At about 9 days the puppies' eyes open. Around the same time they start to get up on their feet and within days they are lurching happily around the box, getting stronger every day. Now is the time to register your litter with the Kennel Club. You will be very unlucky to lose any having reached this age. You obtain the required form from the Kennel Club (see Appendix 1). This has to be countersigned by the owner of the stud dog before being returned with the appropriate fee. At the time of writing, to register a puppy costs £10. If you intend doing the latter you can register an affix with the Kennel Club. This should be done well in advance and, currently, would cost you £45.

When the puppies are 2½ weeks old the holiday is over, for that is what it will have been up to now if all has been normal and straightforward, just fun, enjoying your babies. Now the work begins. The time has come to start them lapping. Make up some milk with whatever powder you have decided to use. Mix the quantity that you require in a small plastic jug and, when ready, stand it in a larger one so that it can be surrounded with hot water to keep it warm. If, at this early age, you offer nearly cold milk, the reaction will be, 'this isn't like mum makes', and you'll have no takers. Try to have a small table in the kennel, about 2 ft 6 in × 1 ft 9 in will be quite big enough, and a stool. The stool is a great saving on the back if you have eight or ten puppies to feed; you can sit and do the job in comfort. Put a little milk, about a tablespoonful, in a saucer or shallow dish with about a ¾ in rim; you don't have as much milk slopped all over the table with a substantial rim. Hold the puppy up with one hand as it is still very wobbly on its legs at this age, and hold the dish in the other. As soon as you put the puppy's nose down to the milk it will splutter a bit and then it will start to lap. You will get the odd puppy that is a problem child but they learn quickly. To begin with, once daily will be sufficient. It is more, at this stage, a matter of teaching them to lap than of meeting an actual need for additional food. As soon as they are lapping with gusto, which is usually after three or four days, introduce your babies to solid food, namely the best quality minced beef – they'll love this! A portion about the size of a walnut is sufficient. I feed it with my finger to start with – it is sucked in rather than eaten normally. When you begin this, give mince in the morning and milk in the afternoon. Increase the quantities of both very slightly each day. By the time the pups are 3½ weeks old you should be able to let two lap from the same bowl. Once the puppies are eating the mince with no problems, introduce a small quantity of Skinner's Puppy Meal, or whatever you have decided to use. If you are using a complete food, rapidly increase the meal and decrease the mince. By the time the puppies are 4 weeks old they should be receiving two solid feeds a day and one of milk, that is, solids at 8.00 a.m., milk at 12.00 noon and solids at 4.00 p.m. The recommended quantity of Skinner's Puppy Meal is ½ oz per 1 lb body weight, divided into however many feeds you wish to give. When the puppies are on the full amount of meal, add 1 oz mince and a little 'soup' to each mix. The latter can be Oxo or something similar. Don't make the feed too sloppy, just wet enough to go down easily. Good feeding is a matter of gentle progression. If you achieve empty bowls, firm motions and expanding puppies, you've got it right! There are so many different foods available these days that it is really a matter of personal choice and following instructions. Some are better than others, but if you stick to one of the better known manufacturers you cannot go far wrong.

From the time when the puppies start to put a real drain on the bitch's resources, watch out for eclampsia (milk fever). It is not common, but it is very possible and, to those who do not know what it is, it is very frightening. In the simplest of terms, it is a calcium deficiency. The fact that you have been feeding calcium throughout the pregnancy does not prevent it. It helps, but there is a limit to the amount that a bitch can absorb into her system. It strikes very quickly. A bitch can be behaving quite normally and within an hour or less will be showing all the signs. If so, she suddenly seems to become dazed and wobbles and stumbles around in the kennel, her eyes glazed. Then she will fall down, tremble violently, start kicking, and in fact give every appearance of having a fit. She will then stiffen. The spasm will pass, only to repeated almost immediately, and it will continue until she is treated. Treatment must be given as quickly as you can get her to your vet, or get him out to you. Don't mess around because if you do your bitch will die. The treatment appears miraculous: an injection of 10 ml of calcium borogluconate and within minutes your bitch, whilst shaken, will be back to normal. In the days when I was involved in cattle, I used to see cows flat out with legs stiff; five minutes after treatment they would get up and walk away, albeit rather unsteadily. Anyway, at the very first symptoms get hold of your vet. After treatment keep the puppies away from the bitch for twelve to twenty-four hours if at all possible. Eclampsia can rear its ugly head soon after whelping, but that is unusual. Normally it will manifest itself when the maximum strain is being put on the bitch. Don't become too alarmed over this, just watchful; I have only experienced about five cases in fifty years.

After four weeks, take the bitch out from the puppies when you feed them in the morning. Let her back for about ten minutes after the midday feed and then out again until around 6.00 p.m. After a further two or three days keep her out until the pups have had a fourth feed, of milk, around 10.00 p.m. To this feed you can add some Weetabix or a small quantity of meal. By the time the puppies are 5 to 5½ weeks old, the bitch should be away from them completely. At this stage they should be receiving a third to a half pint of milk each feed. Now is the time to start grooming. Gently brush and comb them every day. They can get quite messy and, at times, you may find you have to wash them around their tail end. If you have to do this, always make sure that they are properly dry. A sprinkling of Johnson's Baby Powder, when grooming, helps to keep them clean and nice smelling.

Some will not agree with separating the bitch from the puppies, but it is much easier on her. I have seen bitches which were left with their puppies until the latter were 8 to 9 weeks old looking positively emaciated when they have been eventually taken away. In such cases the bitch will almost certainly have dried up but will regurgitate her food for the puppies. Whilst that is natural in the wilds, it is totally unnecessary in the case of a domesticated bitch. Apart from lessening the strain on your girl, weaning the puppies at 5 weeks allows you to regulate their food intake and know exactly what they are receiving. You must watch your bitch very carefully when you do this. Cut her food and water to a minimum and dry her off as quickly as possible. If you feel she is alarmingly full, you may have to let her back to the puppies to suck her out once or twice, but don't do that unless you absolutely have to. Really it is better if you draw some of the milk off by hand, checking her carefully for a few days to make sure she does not develop mastitis. As I have said, there will be those who will not approve of weaning the puppies at 5 weeks. Several years ago I visited the breeding centre for the Guide Dogs to the Blind Association and was informed that whenever possible they take the bitches away from their puppies at 3 weeks!

Feeding continues along the lines already suggested, increasing quantities in ratio to the puppies' growth rate. By the time the puppies are 5 weeks old you can feed them in threes. Should there be a small puppy, or slow feeder, then common sense decrees it is fed on its own.

From about three weeks onwards, the division should be in place in the kennel so that the bitch can escape from her pups when she feels like it. At the same time the rest of the kennel should be made available for the puppies. When this happens, whilst maintaining the Vet-bed in the box, put large sheets of newspaper on the floor and shred paper on to these. The tabloids are the easiest to shred, tearing from the fold. The reason for the shredded paper is that when the pups are moving around they will spread the paper to cover up where they have emptied themselves. When it is time to clean the kennel, you can roll up the paper from one corner and the whole job takes only a matter of minutes. When you take the bitch away completely, put white sawdust on the floor, but retain the Vet-bed, providing the puppies do not start to tear it up. If they do, put straw in the bed.

At 3 weeks you should worm the puppies for round worm with a syrup such as Early Worm or Shirley's to name two. Both are easily obtainable from pet shops. Worm again at five weeks with piperazine citrate, which you will have to obtain from your vet, and repeat this ten days later. When the puppies are $4\frac{1}{2}$ to 5 weeks old, turn the heat off during the day and, providing the weather is nice, let them play in the outside kennel run. At this stage spend as much time as you can with them, pet them and get them to come to you, in fact humanise them. Never be cross or rough with a baby puppy; it should grow up looking upon people as its friend.

From 3 to 4 weeks you should be having prospective buyers visiting to see your puppies. If a person wishes to have one, find out as much as you can about the home and the life it will be leading; remember all I said in the early chapters and don't forget to take full details – name, address and phone number – and to take a deposit. Remember it is now you have to give advice to the beginner and to provide a diet sheet and the relevant papers. The wheel has gone full circle!

APPENDIX 1

Useful Addresses

The Kennel Club. Secretary: Major-General M. H. Sinnatt, CB, 1 Clarges Street, Piccadilly, London W1Y 8AB. Tel. 01–493 6651. Registration Dept: 01–493 2001.

Turner Richards. Cardigan Street, Birmingham B4 7SA. Tel. 021–359 5577.

Allbrooks Products Ltd, 9 Curzon Road, Chilton Industrial Estate, Sudbury, Suffolk CO10 6XW

The Management of Epilepsy in Dogs, by Phyllis G. Croft, PhD, FRCVS, published by Henston, c/o Update-Siebert Publications Ltd, 13–21 High Street, Guildford, Surrey GU1 3DX.

Roger Skinner Ltd. The Mills, Stradbroke, Eye, Suffolk IP21 5HL

APPENDIX 2

BVA/Kennel Club Approved Ophthalmologists
as at 1 January 1998

England
K W BARBER, BvetMed, CertVOphthal, MRCVS
97 Mount Pleasant, Redditch
Worcestershire B97 5QR
Telephone 01527 550111

Dr K C BARNETT, OBE, MA, BSc, DVOphthal, FRCVS, DipECVO
Animal Health Trust, Lanwades Park
Kentford, Newmarket Suffolk CB8 7UU
Telephone 01638 751000

MT BATE, BVM&S, CertVOphthal, MRCVS
Oaks Veterinary Hospital
87 Watford Road, Cotteridge
Birmingham, West Midlands B30 1NP
Telephone 0121 4594333

Professor P G C BEDFORD, BvetMed, PhD, DVOphthal, FRCVS, DipECVO
Royal Veterinary College, Hawkshead Lane
Hatfield, Hertfordshire AL9 7TA
Telephone 01707 666333

N J BURDEN, BVSc CertVOphthal, MRCVS
The Hale Veterinary Group, 19 Langley Road
Chippenham, Wiltshire SN15 1BS
Telephone 01249 65361

Mrs B COTTRELL, MA, VetMB CertVOphthal, MRCVS
Stone Lane Veterinary Hospital
Meldreth, Royston, Hertfordshire SG8 6NZ
Telephone 01763 261457

Dr S M CRISPIN, MA, VetMB BSc,
DVA, DVOphthal, MRCVS, DipECVO
Dept of Clinical Veterinary Science
University of Bristol,
Langford House
Langford, Bristol, Avon BS40 5DU
Telephone 0117 928 9690

S R ELLIS, BVSc, CertVOphthal, MRCVS
Riverbank Veterinary Centre
16/22 Watery Lane, Preston
Lancashire PR2 2NN
Telephone 01772 726745

P J EVANS, MA, VetMB, CertVOphthal, MRCVS
Eye Veterinary Clinic, Moreton Eye
Leominster, Herefordshire HR6 0DP
Telephone 01568 616616

S J FOSTER, BVSc, CertVOphthal MRCVS
The Barton Veterinary Hospital
34 New Dover Road, Canterbury
Kent CT1 3DT
Telephone 01227 765522

K J FRASER, BVM&S, CertVOphthal, MRCVS
37 Caldecott Road, Abingdon
Oxfordshire OX14 5EZ
Telephone 01235 528177

J V GOODYEAR, BVM&S, CertVOphthal, MRCVS
Springwood Veterinary Group
90 Spring Terrace Road
Burton on Trent, Staffordshire DE15 9DX
Telephone 01283 568162

J S HEATH, CertVOphthal, MRCVS
608 Veterinary Group
608 Warwick Road
Solihull, West Midlands B91 1AA
Telephone 0121 705044

M P C LAWTON, BVetMed, CertVOphthal, CertLAS, CBiol, MIBiol, FRCVS
12 Fitzilian Avenue. Harold Wood, Romford, Essex RM3 0QS
Telephone 01708 384444

S J LEWIS, BVSc, CertVOphthal, MRCVS
The Veterinary Centre, 14 Bond End Yoxall
Burton on Trent, Staffordshire DE13 8NH
Telephone 01543 472249

I K MASON, MA, VetMB, CertVOphthal, MRCVS
Seadown Veterinary Hospital
Frost Lane, Hythe, Hants SO45 3NG
Telephone 01703 842237

P McPHERSON, BVMS, CertVOphthal, MRCVS
Minster Veterinary Centre
Orchard Lodge, Newark Road
Southwell, Nottinghamshire NG25 0ES
Telephone 01636 812133

Mrs L J NEWMAN, BVM&S, CertVOphthal, MRCVS
Eye Veterinary Clinic, Moreton Eye,
Leominster, Herefordshire HR6 0DP
Telephone 01568 616616

R PONTEFRACT, BVMS, CertVOphthal, CertEO, MRCVS
43 Empingham Road, Stamford
Lincolnshire PE9 2RJ
Telephone 01780 764333

J D RICKETTS BVM&S, CertVOphthal, MRCVS
Royd Cottage, 38 Sude Hill, New Mill
Huddersfield, West Yorkshire HD7 7BZ
Telephone 01484 682034

P W RENWICK MA VetMB DVOphthal MRCVS
Willows Referral Service, 78 Tanworth Rd
Shirley, Solihull, W. Midlands B90 4DF
Telephone 0121 7451354

Miss J SANSOM, BVSc, DVOphthal, MRCVS
Animal Health Trust, Lanwades Park
Kentford, Newmarket, Suffolk CB8 7UU
Telephone 01638 751000

Dr F G STARTUP, BSc, DVOphthal, MRCVS, DipECVO
West Mount, Hambrook Hill
Nr Chichester, Sussex PO18 8UQ
Telephone 01243 572932

S TURNER MA, VetMB, DVOphthal MRCVS
The Mandeville Veterinary Hospital
15 Mandeville Road, Northolt
Middlesex UB5 5HD
Telephone 0181 845 5677

C G B WARREN, BA, VetMB, CertVOphthal, MRCVS
Westmoor Veterinary Centre, Brook Lane
Tavistock, Devon PL19 9BA
Telephone 01822 612561

J J YELLOWLEY, BVSc, CertVOphthal, MRCVS
Rosemount Veterinary Hospital
24 Old Woking Road, West Byfleet, Surrey
KT14 6HP
Telephone 01932 341058

Scotland

M G DAVIDSON, BVM&S, CertVOphthal, MRCVS
19 Hillhouse Road, Edinburgh EH4 3QP
Telephone 0131 3320458

A T McKENZIE, BVMS, CertVOphthal, MRCVS
McKenzie, Bryson & Marshall MsRCVS
21 Hill Street, Kilmarnock
Ayrshire KA3 1HA
Telephone 01563 522701

J R B MOULD, BA, BVSc, DVOphthal, MRCVS
Veterinary School
Bearsden, Glasgow G61 1QH
Telephone 0141 3305700

APPENDIX

A E WALL, BVM&S, CertVOphthal, MSc, MRCVS
Fish Vet Group, 39 Carsegate Road
Inverness IV3 6LL Telephone 01463 717774

Channel Isles

D HABIN, BVM&S, DVOphthal, MRCVS
Route Isabelle Veterinary Practice
Route Isabelle, St Peter Port
Guernsey, Channel Isles GY1 1QR
Telephone 01481 723863

Wales

J L CORMIE, BVMS, CertVOphthal, MRCVS
229 High Street, Blackwood
Gwent NP2 1AL
Telephone 01495 222383

Mrs G E HUBBARD, BvetMed, CertVOphthal, MRCVS
Cibyn Veterinary Clinic, Llanberis Road
Caernarfon, Gwynedd LL55 2BD
Telephone 01286 673026

H R WILLIAMS, BVSc, CertVOphthal, MRCVS
Moat Village Farm
New Moat, Clarbeston Road
Haverfordwest, Pembrokeshire SA63 4RH
Telephone 01437 532274

Northern Ireland

W D J McCARTNEY, BSc, CertVOphthal, MRCVS
Cedar Grove Veterinary Clinic
132 Upper Knockbreda Road
Belfast BT6 9QB
Telephone 01232 703818

I MILLAR, BVMS, CertVOphthal, MRCVS
Earlswood Veterinary Hospital
193 Belmont Road, Belfast BT4 2AE
Telephone 01232 471361

199

Eire

Dr T D GRIMES, BvetMed., DVR, DVOphthal, MRCVS, DipECVO
Faculty of Veterinary Medicine
University College Dublin, Veterinary College
Dublin 4 Eire
Telephone 003531 6687988

APPENDIX 3

Golden Retriever Clubs

The various clubs are listed below, but in view of the fact that club secretaries change and, therefore, any name and addresses given could easily be out of date, none are given, but current ones should be easily available from The Kennel Club.

All-Ireland Golden Retriever Club.
Berkshire Downs & Chiltern Golden Retriever Club.
Eastern Counties Golden Retriever Club.
Midland Golden Retriever Club.
Southern Golden Retriever Association.
Northern Golden Retriever Association.
Golden Retriever Club of Northumbria.
North West Golden Retriever Club.
Golden Retriever Club of Scotland.
Southern Golden Retriever Society.
Southwestern Golden Retriever Club.
Ulster Golden Retriever Club.
Golden Retriever Club of Wales.
Yorkshire Golden Retriever Club.

APPENDIX 4

Insurance

Dog Breeders' Insurance Co Ltd, 12 Christchurch Road, Lansdowne, Bournemouth, BH1 3LE. Tel. 0202 295771.
Pet Plan Ltd, 319–27 Chiswick High Road, London W4 4HH. Tel. 01–995 5281.
Protect-A-Pet Ltd, 15 Knightsbridge Green, London SW1X 7QL. Tel. 01–581 0187.

APPENDIX 5

Conditions of Sale.

I, the Buyer, ... agree to purchase the Golden Retriever puppy, ... , KC Registration Number .... from the Seller for the sum of £ ....

The Buyer, having examined certificates in respect of Hereditary Eye Diseases, Hip Dysplasia and other such documents as may be available applicable to the parents of the above puppy, as issued by a qualified veterinary surgeon, accept that such certificates do not in any way constitute a Warranty, but are purely an opinion given at the time of examination by the veterinary surgeon, as the said puppy, being a living creature, cannot carry a guarantee that could be applicable to an inanimate object.

The Seller undertakes that the puppy, at the time of sale is in good health and corresponds to the description as given by the Seller and that all other warranties, conditions or terms relating to the said puppy, whether implied by statute or common law or otherwise are excluded.

The Seller agrees that, on being notified of any problem, the Buyer may return the puppy within one calendar month from the date of purchase, providing the Buyer presents a veterinary surgeons certificate stating that the puppy was suffering from a condition that was to it's detriment at the time of purchase. Given such circumstances the Seller will be responsible for the veterinary surgeons fee.

Notwithstanding this Condition of Sale the Seller's liability to the Buyer, whether for any breach of the Conditions of Sale or otherwise, shall not in any event exceed the Price and the Seller shall be under no liability for any direct loss and/or expense or indirect loss and/or expense suffered by the Buyer or liability to third parties incurred by the Buyer.

Signature of Buyer ....

Address. ....

....

....

....

Signature of Seller ....

Address..

....

....

....

Date. ....